Stories

FROM THE

Hole in the Ceiling

Stories
FROM THE
Hole in the Ceiling

ANNE GALWAY

FLANKER PRESS LIMITED
ST. JOHN'S

Library and Archives Canada Cataloguing in Publication

Stories from the hole in the ceiling / Anne Galway.

Also issued in electronic format.
ISBN 978-1-926881-43-0

1. Newfoundland and Labrador--Social life and customs.
2. Newfoundland and Labrador--Anecdotes. I. Galway, Anne, 1939-

FC2168.S76 2011   971.8   C2011-905938-X

© 2011 by Anne Galway

ALL RIGHTS RESERVED. No part of the work covered by the copyright hereon may be reproduced or used in any form or by any means—graphic, electronic or mechanical—without the written permission of the publisher. Any request for photocopying, recording, taping, or information storage and retrieval systems of any part of this book shall be directed to Access Copyright, The Canadian Copyright Licensing Agency, 1 Yonge Street, Suite 800, Toronto, ON M5E 1E5. This applies to classroom use as well.

PRINTED IN CANADA

Edited by Iona Bulgin
Cover art by Anne Galway
Illustrations by Janice Udell
Cover Design: Adam Freake

FLANKER PRESS LTD.
PO BOX 2522, STATION C
ST. JOHN'S, NL
CANADA

TELEPHONE: (709) 739-4477   FAX: (709) 739-4420   TOLL-FREE: 1-866-739-4420
WWW.FLANKERPRESS.COM

15 14 13 12 11   1 2 3 4 5 6 7 8

We acknowledge the financial support of the Government of Canada through the Book Publishing Industry Development Program (BPIDP) for our publishing activities; the Canada Council for the Arts which last year invested $20.1 million in writing and publishing throughout Canada; the Government of Newfoundland and Labrador, Department of Tourism, Culture and Recreation.

Contents

Map: Locations of Stories from the Hole in the Ceiling ix
Introduction 1

Chapter 1: Jam Jams 5

The Hole and the Jam Jams *Dolores Hynes* 7
After the Fire *T. Lopez* 10
Rescue Accomplished *Pearl George* 11
Murder Hunt on PEI *Donna Marie Kelly* 12
Tinkle, Tinkle ... *"Esau"* 14
The Imp! *Ina Belcher* 15
Nosy Parkers *Erika Peddle* 16
The Brick *Catherine Peters* 18
Clean Socks? *Rick Barnes* 20
Thirty-four Eyes *Betty Ryan* 23
The Register *Foster Thornhill* 24
What Do You See? *Louise Fournier* 25
On a String *Beulah Inkpen* 27
Oops! *Beulah Morgan* 28
The Hole Secret *Ron Pumphrey* 29

Chapter 2: Lessons Learned 33

Lessons Learned *Dolo Lee* 35
The Stove between Them *Jolene Gladney* 36

v

The Whole Picture *Sherry Pilgrim-Simms* 37
The Hooked Mat *Unsigned* 42
The Hockey Game *Rex Colbourne* 43
The Hatch *Paul Martin* 44
Blueberry Muffins and Raisin Buns *Maureen Ryan* 47
Uncle Doff Goes to the East Indies *JoAnna Bennett* 48
The Kitchen *Geraldine Keough* 50
No Holes Barred *Angela Otto* 51
The Sleepwalker *Ethel Chaulk* 53
Making Popcorn *Minnie Goodyear* 54
The Powers through the Ages *Celine Power Kear* 56
Properly Set *Barbara Brennan* 58
Caught in the Act *Agatha McDonald* 59

Chapter 3: Buttons, Buttons ... I Found the Buttons 61

Buttons ... Buttons ... I Found the Buttons *Anne Galway* 63
Ragtime Annie *Phillip Pardy* 75
"Marnin Faultin!" *Clarence and Sarah Dewling* 77
The Drool *Dianne (Aucoin) Walsh* 79
Them Days *Emma Martin* 80
Wet Hair Tells the Tale *Marilyn Billard* 81
We Two *Mary (Collins) Walsh and Doris Collins-Scott* 83
Seen and Not Heard *Anita Pender* 85
"Santa Here Yet?" *Dorothy Fitzgerald* 87
Need to Go *Maryanne Drake* 89
"Can a Woman Who Was Once Loved Completely ..."
   Theresa Cantwell 90
Holding Her Own *Joyce and Alan Macpherson* 91
The Internet *Joseph W. Roberts* 92
Sagging Stockings *Alice Lee Finn* 93
The Old Anglican Rectory *Gail Snook* 94
Dancing on the Bridge *Donna Marie Kelly* 96

Chapter 4: The Townie Learns Her Lesson 99

The Townie Learns Her Lesson *Mabel Kean* 101
Hockey Night in Canada *Donna Judge Malarsky* 105
All Around The Circle *Darlene Antle* 106
Tricky Memories *Dolores Bedingfield* 109
Rough Landing *Patricia Power* 111
Five Hundreds *Anne Murrin Walker* 112
Hanging *Steven Shears and Dallis Shears* 113
Taking Turns *Vera Frampton* 114
Uncle Am and the Priest *Kathy Lee* 115
Look at Me! *Peter Breen* 117
Memories Are Made of This *Gloria J. McHugh* 118
Off the Rocker *Gordon Dalton* 120
Gentle Rain *Daphne King* 121
Airborne *Patricia Kean* 122
He Knows ... *Elizabeth Ridgley* 123
Leaving for Boston *Anne Galway* 124

Chapter 5: Portal Antics 127

Portal Antics *J. Pius Bennett* 129
The American Factor *Rhonda Peddle* 131
Company *Roger Willmott* 132
The Scuttle *Tony Strong* 135
The Pail *Jeanette Holwell* 136
The Comfort Stove *Owen Brown* 137
The IWA Strike *Gary Collins* 138
Winter Logans *Ed Norman* 140
After School *Myrtle Tippett* 142
Burnt Toast Remedy *Donna Winsor* 144
Life's Lessons *Eileen Keating* 145
The Cozy Hole *Isabel Croke* 147
Mischief *George J. Sturge* 148
Rescue Aborted *Pearl George* 149

Bum Start *Lorraine Croft* 150
Elizabeth and Archie Get Married *A. Dominix* 152

Chapter 6: The "Hole" Truth 155

The "Hole" Truth *Connie Peddle* 157
Up the Depot *Marjorie Fudge* 160
The Listening Post *Reta Phillips* 163
Scars *Eric White* 164
Cooking Lessons *Ron Hammond* 165
Moving In *Gary Snow* 166
Shortcut *Gerry Sulley* 167
Give Us This Day ... *Phyllis Mary Smith* 168
Fishing through the Hole *Guy Randell* 169
The Peep Hole in the Ceiling *Madonna M. Rideout* 170
The Dance *Annie and Reg King* 172
Spies *Peggy Doyle* 173
Found Out *Rosalie Quinn* 174
Yeast and Malt *Judy Shortt* 175
The Secret *Beulah Gillingham* 176

Acknowledgements 177
Index of Contributors 181

Locations of Stories from the Hole in the Cailing

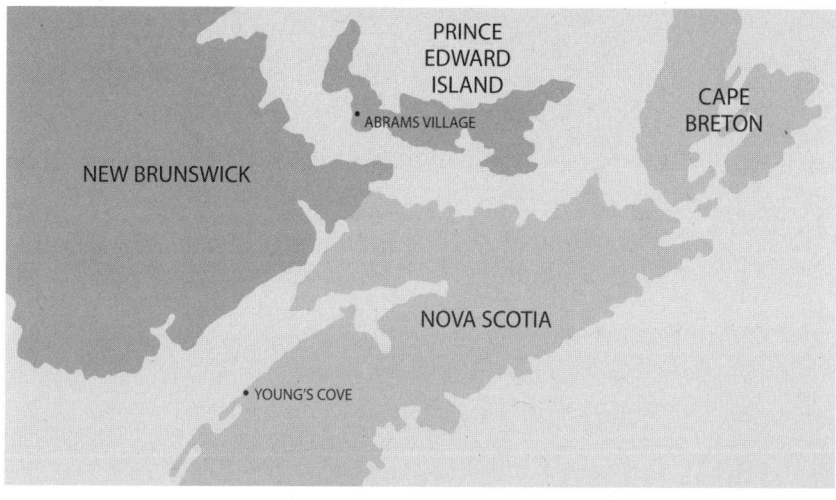

Introduction

> *Many of life's lessons were taught and many of life's lessons were learned through the hole in the kitchen ceiling.*
>
> MABEL KEAN

> *The hole in the ceiling sure meant that life during hard times was just a little bit more bearable.*
>
> ANITA PENDER (NEE CHEESEMAN)

The stories gathered here belong mostly to the era of the 1940s and 50s, although some of them reveal that the hole in the kitchen ceiling still resonates today.

This collection confirms that the hole in the kitchen ceiling provided a source of heat in Newfoundland homes from Conception Bay to Port aux Basques and from St. Anthony to St. Lawrence on the Burin Peninsula. The stories were written by people of all ages, men and women, Newfoundlanders at home, and in places as far away as Alberta, Winnipeg, Toronto, New York, New Brunswick, and New Hampshire.

For many years, I wanted to paint a picture of my memory of the hole, but I didn't know how to paint. I took lessons and, in 1995, I completed the painting *Balcony View*. When I brought the painting to a local frame shop, the proprietor remarked that he, too, remembered a story about the hole in the ceiling of his house, which he related then and there. When other friends and family saw this image, I heard their stories. From there, I thought it would be a worthwhile project to collect and share these stories.

Working with so many people has been a wonderful experience. I shared life stories with strangers, and I was astonished at the generosity of people willing to help with the collation of these stories. I benefitted from the expertise of publishers, professional writers, amateur photographers, and, most of all, the story-writers in this book.

No restrictions were placed on writers except that their stories had to have some relevance to the hole. Many writers gave colourful descriptions of the typical Newfoundland home. Cultural traditions such as "Marnin Faultin" on St. Valentine's Day were revisited. Other stories were embellished to entertain in true Newfoundland fashion, exaggerating dialogue but always retaining the point of view from the hole. Just as pertinent were the single incident stories, which included wonderful images of the courtin' couple, rings of cigarette smoke, a bum in the hole to be inspected, and children as spies.

Childhood accidents, such as falling through the hole and mistaking the hole for the toilet, were recounted. Christmas experiences were a source of joy (and sometimes sorrow). Other major life events—pregnancies, family members leaving home, deaths—were often learned through the hole.

A small snapshot-in-time of our Newfoundland history has been captured and preserved. The feature in common, the hole in the ceiling, was the instrument through which we viewed our unique society.

As we warmed our bodies, many facets of our social and intellectual beings were also being addressed. While I do not hope to capture all the nuances of Newfoundland living in this collection, stories of the hole covered such aspects of life as family entertainment, religion, learning from one another, respect for all generations of families, the work people did, and the everlasting importance of storytelling.

Sometimes the hole presented children with a view of a larger world as they heard about the IWA strike in Bishop's Falls, Hitler, and World War II. Other writers took solace in revisiting the loss of relatives when they didn't understand how life and death worked. For some writers, it was enough that they had enjoyed writing their childhood memories and had at last preserved them for their families. Whether written with professional expertise or from the view of the first-time writer with a story to tell, the authors' efforts are equally valued.

As much as possible, these stories are preserved in the writers' own voices and have only been lightly edited to set the tone of this collection.

While many stories typical of past experiences are preserved here, there are many more to be told. If you are so moved to write and share, I invite you to join the almost one hundred people who have already provided fodder to jog our memories and be part of our history's preservation.

ANNE GALWAY

Send stories to:

64 Neptune Road
St. John's NL
A1B 4J3

or email:
galwayja@nf.sympatico.ca

CHAPTER 1

Jam Jams

I'd offer you something sweet, but ...

☞ The Hole and the Jam Jams ☜

EACH NOOK AND CRANNY and the objects held within played a prominent role in the life of our kitchen. The polka-dot linoleum marked the year Grandfather died, and a concoction of saintly images, including a large likeness of the Sacred Heart of Jesus, perched over a perpetual light, defined our beliefs. A pine cupboard, painted cream, displayed an array of oddities—breakable roosters and miniature teapots—while the daybed with its frilly covers hid hordes of treasures waiting to be rediscovered. The table, a vantage point for news, provided space for supper-eating, card-playing, baby-washing, and lesson-learning, while the rocking chair coaxed youngsters through the Boo-man, running ears, and colic. The NAFCO Special was the pride of the kitchen. Besides scalding cream and baking bread, the old black and white stove dried quilts, hatched out chickens, thawed out perishing lambs, and, one time, incubated a premature baby. The green chair near the stove blistered and peeled, and, from above it, stared the hole.

The hole had a life of its own and served its purpose well. This opening was no accident: it was cut just the right size, trimmed with mouldings and painted on the inside. Looking up, one could see the patterned piece of canvas or rag mat. The hole not only let heat into Mother's room but it was the eyes and ears of the upstairs, an instrument of voyeurism to the kitchen downstairs.

Although from the hole I could see only bits and pieces of the kitchen, I did see who came in, who went out, what was being poked into the cupboard, and I could hear every word. A visitor would usually sit on the green chair under the hole, and because Mother had acquired a selective deafness from a bout of scarlet fever in her younger years, tuning in was easy. Since my bed lay near the foot of Mother's and near the hole, my bedtime stories were not of princesses or talking bears but of who had the most fish salted, who was working in Goose Bay, and who had married a Yank. Verses of "Mary of the Wild Moor" or "Mother's Old Checkered Apron" lulled me to sleep. To get a better look or a clearer sound I would lie on the floor by the hole and, depending on the talk of the kitchen, would fall asleep in the sweltering heat of my burrow. Of course, I was constantly reminded to heed the "code of the hole" but, for the life of me, I could never think of anything worth repeating.

While the hole was a unique intercom system, it also served as a time saver. Items could be passed through the hole—underwear, the iron, a drink, a set of teeth, the cat. However, when the boy across the meadow, in the presence of "mortified" visitors from St. John's, stuck his bum in the hole asking to be wiped, the hole protocol had to be revisited.

Now I cannot mention the antic of the bum without confessing to a hole-related misdemeanour of my own. Mother had sent me on the weekly bill-paying mission to the Co-Op store on the north side. Since it was Saturday, I dilly-dallied, being every bit as lackadaisical as Mother said I was. Having spent my twenty cents on a bottle of lime, a bag of cheesies, and a cherry popsicle, and having carried on with some friends, I set out for the long trek back up the bay. I traipsed along until I could no longer stand the brick-like weight of the brown paper bag and, since I was halfway home, I decided to take a spell on Ryan's Bank. I played on the lookout rock, picked flowers, and watched someone mowing hay. Believe me, I had no intention of inspecting the contents of the bag but, to make a long story short, I had inside a whole pack of Purity Jam Jams. I couldn't eat just one, I thought, or even a row, so once I started there was no going back. I would throw the wrapping over the Gut Bridge and the absence of the Jam Jams would go unnoticed.

Hours later when I handed Mother the bag, she already had the look—the Examine-Your-Conscience look, the Act-of-Contrition look. She placed each item on the kitchen table—the can of corn, the tin of peaches, the carton of tobacco—and folded up what was left of the brown paper bag. Then she read the note attached to the receipt, the note with the words of betrayal that I had carried all the way home: "Clara, no Export tobacco only Target, last pack of Jam Jams until truck comes, Bertie." I knew my punishment would be the litany of the note. My stomach felt queasy as I lay my head on the mat near the hole.

Voices from the hole awakened me in the darkened room and waves of heat struck me in the face. I could hear Mother remarking on Mr. Bill's new hat, a quiff he had bought at Ayre and Sons. I could see the colourful feather on the right side tucked into the band and the dip in the top that reminded me of the inside of a dory. "I'd offer you something sweet …" Mother started, but before she could finish, down the hole spewed lumps and chunks of green, orange, red, and brown. Mr. Bill's hat would never be the same. Remnants of cheese sticks and Jam Jams had lodged in the brim and in the dory-like quiff, and any liquid remainder of my excursion had trickled down the poor man's neck.

The Sweet Marie bar Mr. Bill had brought for me remained in the cupboard for weeks and a nickel a day was all I got for the shop. Jam Jams were not on the Co-Op order for a long while. Shortly after the hole episode, I graduated from the single bed in Mother's room to the three-quarter bed in the spare room, a paltry room with little opportunity for mischief but located directly across the hall from the hole. The orifice of the upstairs, the gateway to the kitchen, the hole would continue to play an integral part.

Dolores Hynes
CALVERT

After the Fire

I AM A MEMBER of a family of eight—six boys, my mother, and my father. We lived in a home in Botwood where there was a hole in the ceiling covered with a grate.

I remember when we moved to this house, after we lost our other home to a big fire. When we moved into this new house, it felt warm and cozy. We had my grandmother come and stay with us for the summer. I was her pet. Everyone said, "Look at you. Nan's pet. You get what you want, always."

Anyway, I am getting away from the subject. We went into the house and started investigating and seeing what awesome things we could find. I ran through the hall, bounded up the stairs, got to the top, out of breath and all. I stopped dead in my tracks, as there it was: the hole in the ceiling. I remember the grate covering it, and the heat coming from the wood stove.

On Christmas Eve that same year our parents sent us to bed before Santa came. My brothers and I went to sleep. But a little later, I remember waking up to hear noises coming from downstairs. I looked down through the grate and saw my mother and my father in the midst of decorating our home for Christmas. I watched and watched for what seemed like hours as they worked diligently getting ready for the holiday season. When they finally finished, I could see the most beautiful Christmas tree in the corner. It looked awesome. We had thought that we weren't going to be able to have a tree for Santa to present us with gifts.

Christmas morning came, and we all ran down the stairs. We were amazed by the tree. It was beautiful. I felt overwhelmed. It was decorated with bright lights and had chocolates as ornaments, as we really didn't have much money. We limbed the tree of all chocolates. Mom and Dad, who were not impressed, scolded us big time. Still, it was a great looking tree. To this day, Mom still talks about it, and we all smile.

T. Lopez
ST. JOHN'S

❧ Rescue Accomplished ☙

A FEW YEARS AFTER I left my home in Hickman's Harbour on Random Island, my parents had a new ceiling put in the kitchen. The old hole was replaced by a new square hole with a vent. My two children loved to visit Nan and loved lying on the floor peeping through the vent at anyone below.

At the time we had a Labrador dog named Blackie. The kids drove Blackie crazy talking to him through the vent. He didn't know where they were and would become quite scared. One morning when they were tormenting him, he ran up the stairs and was afraid to come down.

As Nan would be crazy to see a dog upstairs, they came running to me to help get the dog back downstairs. Yelling only made the dog worse. In a panic to get him down before Nan showed, I raced up the stairs, picked up the seventy-pound dog and started down the narrow stairs. The poor dog was so scared that he spread his paws and banged each stair rail on the way down.

The kids still laugh about how funny it was to see their mother carrying Blackie, and how I afterwards forbade them to ever go near that darn vent in the ceiling.

Pearl George
MOUNT PEARL

Murder Hunt on PEI

Marcie and I lay flattened to the floor, eyes and nose pressed on the heat vent, a hole in the floor of Grannie's house that allowed the heat to rise upstairs.

"Fifteen two, fifteen four and a pair is six!" says Grandpa.

We watch Uncle Ephram move a matchstick over the crib board and stand it into the hole.

The radio crackles, but continues to play. "Say, hey good lookin', watcha got cookin'?" Marcie and I bob our heads to the music. I bump my nose against the vent and we snort bursts of air through our noses to keep from giggling out loud.

The dusty heat from the wood stove brushes our faces. Our toes tingle from being flattened against the cool linoleum floor.

"Fifteen two, fifteen four, fifteen six, fifteen eight and a pair for ten," says Uncle Gerald, laughing loudly.

Grannie moves the matchstick for him with her thin, wrinkled hands. I see the blue network of veins that stand from her skin like the bumps on a globe.

"Shhh! Listen," says Uncle Gerald, pointing to the radio.

"... interrupt this program for a special news bulletin. A tragic event has taken place in Abrams Village, Egmont Bay, earlier this evening. Two people were murdered in their homes. The suspect is still at large. There is widespread fear throughout the community this evening as police search a wooded area, close to the murder scene."

"Oh my God!" says Grannie, blessing herself.

"I've got to get home," says Uncle Ephram. "Rita and the children are alone."

Grampa walks him to the door. "I'll make sure the door is locked and I'll watch until you get to your house," he says.

"I'll get on the party line and see what I can find out," says Uncle Gerald, heading for the phone.

Emma, the maid, runs to check the windows.

Marcie and I lock eyes. Hers are wide, and eyebrows raised. Her lips are stretched as if she is about to scream, but nothing escapes her lips. I think that my own face mirrors hers. We are interrupted by more sounds from below. Our eyes drop back to the hole.

"It's true. It's Jack and Madeline who've been murdered," says Uncle Gerald.

Grannie's head drops into her arm. Grampa slumps into his chair.

With a look between us, Marcie and I run for the stairs and barrel down. We run into Grannie's arms, laying our heads into her lap, babbling and crying. She tries to calm us. Much later we agree to go to bed with Emma. We make her hang a blanket over the window.

It is only as I'm drifting off to sleep that I remembered that nothing was said to us about spying through the hole in the floor.

Donna Marie Kelly
MIDDLE COVE

❧ Tinkle, Tinkle ... ☙

In the late 1940s before central heating, there was a grated hole beside the bed in my sister's room. It was also in the days when toilets were outside where they belonged and urgent needs were satisfied by a pot underneath the bed.

One evening, my sister, the youngest, had gone to bed, while the remainder of the family, including the teacher who was boarding with us, were relaxing in the front room. My little sister, awakened by a call of nature, struggled sleepily out of her bed and, seeing the pale glimmer emanating from the grate, assumed it was the pot. Squatting above the vent, she showered the stove in the room below.

The odour was indescribable, and the astonishment of those in the room was no less so. It slowly dawned on my parents what had happened and we boys thought it was hilarious.

Today, that event is never mentioned in our sister's presence. It would destroy the family's cohesion to do so, but I think it's too good to be forgotten entirely.

"Esau"
Eastport

Name withheld at the author's request

૭ THE IMP! ૭

HOW WELL I REMEMBER the hole in the ceiling of my home in St. John's. My sister and I watched Mom and her club friends play many games of cards. When they finished, they had a cup of tea and sandwiches or cookies as they shared their news, whether happy or sad.

My only brother, Harold, was ten years younger than me. He was a real imp. Anyway, one Christmas when I was around sixteen, I was allowed to help fill his stocking. Mom, Dad and I were in the kitchen because it was too cold in the living room where earlier we had decorated the tree. While I examined the toys which my mother brought into the kitchen from their hiding places, she remembered a special one she had bought for my little brother.

"I'll be right back," she said, rushing off to get a large wooden sleigh from under the stairs in the hall.

As I removed his stocking from the top of the warmer oven, I heard a voice from the hole above.

"Hi, Santa!"

At that point I felt like putting coal in his stocking.

Every Christmas this story brings a few chuckles as it gets told again and again. My brother has passed on due to an automobile accident, which gives me all the more reason to treasure this memory.

Ina Belcher (nee Brown)
TONAWANDA, NEW YORK

ಌ Nosy Parkers ⋘

In August 2009, my grandfather Joseph Abbott passed away after suffering with cancer for a short period of time. He was known to many as Uncle Joe and was nothing less than a "jack of all trades." He was an amazing person, and anyone who knew him would agree. My grandmother, Blanche Abbott, had resided in St. John's in their new home for the past few years.

Not one day goes by that I don't think of their small white and red house by the water in New Perlican. My heart swells with pride to think of Nan's flowers in the garden and Granddad's creations in the yard, everything handmade and perfect in most eyes. At night, the routine was always the same. We piled around to play checkers on Granddad's homemade checkerboard table, play cards, or have a snack of Nan's homemade toast with butter. Sometimes if we were lucky, we could sneak some of Nan's famous chocolate cake before bedtime.

After kisses goodnight, my sister, my brother and I would head upstairs to bed. The backroom always enchanted me. After my siblings were asleep, I would lie by the hole in the ceiling in the backroom. Grown-up talk always intrigued my wildest imagination. Every once in a while I would hear creaks from the stairs and hop back up into bed as quietly as possible, hoping no one knew I was awake.

I remember looking down through the hole at Granddad drinking a small glass of Lamb's and laughing with everyone. One time I remember looking through the hole and Nan looking up and saying, "I see you, Erika." Sometimes I wonder if they knew I was there all along. I wasn't very discreet as I tried to avoid the creaking in walking those couple of steps from the bed to the hole in the ceiling. It was like my own little "nosy heaven" where no one would ever know how my imagination ran free. I loved listening to their stories like "Remember when ..." or listening to their discussions about things I could never understand, no matter how much I wished to—trouting days, berry-picking days, fisherman days, up the shore, and across the barrens.

Now I like to think that Granddad is looking down at the world through a "nosy heaven." Everyday I wake up knowing he will be there in his own hole in the ceiling watching me as I grow.

Erika Peddle
MOUNT PEARL

∽ The Brick ∾

I grew up in the small community of Plate Cove East on the Bonavista peninsula. Far more people lived there then than do nowadays. Most of the older homes were two-storey dwellings. I grew up in a bungalow, so I didn't know much about two-storey houses.

One day I went next door with a friend to visit her grandmother and uncle. Another friend, who also lived in a bungalow, came there looking for us. Most two-storey houses had all the doors closed, especially in winter, to keep the heat in the kitchen. There was a door leading into the kitchen from the porch and one leading to the hall at the foot of the stairs. The wood stove that was used for cooking, baking, and heating the area was connected to an inside brick chimney by funnels. There were no prefab chimneys in those days. Most two-storey houses had a brick chimney in the kitchen and one in the living room. The fire in the living room was rarely lit and, of course, the door leading in there was closed. Everyone gathered in the kitchen.

Meals were prepared, cooked, and served in the kitchen. Most all other activities, like homework, were carried out there, too. Most kitchens in those two-storey homes were painted a cream colour and had wooden beams in the ceiling. Some kitchens were cream colour on the top, a wainscot and the lower part painted green. There was usually a brick chimney, a rocking chair, and two windows. There was also a woodbox for storing wood for the fire. Most kitchens had a built-in stand or a dresser to store the dishes. Some homes had a pantry off the kitchen.

Of course, by the chimney in all those houses was a hole in the ceiling.

My friend's uncle usually sat by the window in the front, by the end of the table. My friend, whom I'll call Marie, needed to go upstairs to get something. Her uncle told her to pass down "that thing" when she went upstairs. So being curious, like all other children, we couldn't wait to see what he was talking about.

We heard Marie call out from upstairs, "Here it is."

We looked towards the chimney where her voice was coming from. She passed down a brick through the hole in the ceiling. Of course, never having seen this before, our eyes were glued to the brick to see what he would do with it. Much to our surprise, he put it in the oven and heated it. Then when it was heated, it was wrapped in a towel and given to Marie to bring back upstairs to put in her uncle's bed to heat it up before he went to bed. Needless to say, we were afraid to look at each other in case we would blow up from laughing and end up in trouble.

Catherine Peters
Knights Cove

❧ Clean Socks? ❦

"**Do I have any** clean socks?"

It's not a question that should stand out from the millions of snatches of conversation I had overheard during my childhood. But when the question is asked by an inverted head suspended over an oil stove cluttered with bubbling pots, it is not easy to forget.

The hole was a practical measure to relieve some of the heat generated by the kitchen stove and funnel it upwards to warm the second floor. The hole in the ceiling, I remember, was at 3 Allan Square in St. John's—my grandmother's house. Number 3 is still there, but the house looks quite different and I imagine the hole is long gone.

The sock-seeker was my uncle, Stan. He was a young adult living with his parents, my grandparents, when I was a preschooler. Stan's head-down approach had the desired effect. It sent my grandmother hunting for socks, fearing he would somehow burn his head or inadvertently drop a dirty sock into the gravy fixings.

The house was a narrow, wooden two-storey that was completely detached, which was a little unusual in that area at the time. It was old, even back in the early 1960s. It was originally my great-grandparents' home and, at some point, my grandparents started a family there, too. They grew into a family of seven and continued sharing the old house with my grandmother's parents.

Back then, it wasn't unusual for houses to be filled to capacity. Economically, it was a practical arrangement, and the children had the added benefit of living with their grandparents under the same roof. Nan and Pop, too, watched their grandchildren grow up and played an active role in their lives. Kids like me, the great-grandchildren, loved to visit the multi-generational house that teemed with ideas and points of view from all quarters.

Looking at it from the street, the house was typical, with a great first-floor bay window that bowed outward over the sidewalk. It sported many coats of thick, dark red oil paint, rendered even darker by the soot of smokey coal fires vented by chimneys all along the street. Everywhere there were sticky black dots, evidence of the many coats of tar applied regularly to keep the flat roof watertight.

Entering from the street, the stairs were on the right, living room on the left, next left was the dining room—each with its own fireplace. At the back was the huge kitchen, growing at odd angles wider than the front of the house and reaching almost to a small vacant lot on Balsam Street. In the sprawling kitchen you could see that the house had been expanded to meet the needs of the growing family.

Upstairs, over the front door, was the bathroom. Over the living room was the master bedroom with an ornate fireplace, then a second bedroom with a fireplace. At the back end of the upstairs hall, over the kitchen, extra rooms had been added at a new level. Two steps down took you to another bedroom. This room had a door at the back opening onto another bedroom— "shotgun style," as they say of the long narrow houses in New Orleans that feature connected rooms. At the back of the adjoining bedroom was yet another door that opened onto a room resting on posts—appropriately called the backroom. This backroom looked out over the house of my grandmother's brother Jack on the far side of Balsam Street.

The front of the house was heated by two oil-fired hall stoves, one in the upstairs hall and one downstairs, and fireplaces, each with its bucket of coal and fireplace tools standing by. The only source of heat for the back of the house was the giant kitchen oil range; so the obvious solution to heat the upstairs was the hole in the kitchen ceiling.

The ceiling hole seems to have served its purpose. I have many memories of the rambling old house on Allan Square, but I don't remember ever feeling cold there. It was an adventure to explore the nooks and crannies of the many closets and odd-shaped corners. Sometimes I sat on the stairs and watched my grandfather and great-grandfather play cards in the dining room in a dense fog of cigarette smoke.

I don't remember ever discovering the top side of the hole in the bedroom over the kitchen, so I didn't have the chance to spy on the kitchen goings-on. But it was a great source of wonder and entertainment on the occasions that I was in the kitchen below when Stan's head popped down through with "What's for dinner?" or "Who's down there?"

Besides table and chairs, the giant kitchen was furnished with a wood and leather couch, called a daybed, and a washing machine. A door opened onto the backyard, and you could access Balsam Street—handy, if you were headed that way. The kitchen was by far the busiest room in the house, functioning as kitchen, dining room for most meals, laundry room, and pantry. The oil stove provided hot water for the house, too, so the exposed boiler and associated piping were painted and accepted as part of the kitchen décor.

In the fall, Stan would take his head out of the ceiling and somehow manage to navigate his Harley-Davidson from Balsam Street into the kitchen for secure winter storage. I remember well the incongruous sight of my grandmother calmly singing to herself while ironing, then folding and piling the endless laundry onto the seat of the silent motorcycle.

Houses today are so much more than shelter. They are huge investments, showpieces, the most obvious indicator of the owner's wealth and status. All the components—stairs, doors and cabinets—are crafted and installed by specialists. The days of a house being owner-adapted to suit the needs of a family, with function overriding aesthetics, are perhaps gone forever. You just don't get together with friends and relatives to build a room on stilts at the back of a million-dollar house.

Houses today, a key element of the family business plan, are ready to be traded whenever the market and the rates are favourable. The heyday of the hole in the ceiling and the "shotgun house," where inexpensive and practical solutions outranked the need for privacy and independence, are behind us. But these sprawling odd-shaped houses were home to three and four generations of family at a time, and helped shape them—for better or worse. The effects of lifestyle changes like this are difficult to calculate.

I don't have a hole in the kitchen ceiling of my house. But I did learn a few things from my head-down Uncle Stan. I can nurse my motorcycle through the rec room door, so it spends winters indoors, near the laundry room. I pile my clean laundry on it, too.

Rick Barnes
St. John's

Thirty-four Eyes

Our hole in the ceiling was located above the living room of our two-storey home on Bell Island. It had a grate over it so that none of us—there were seventeen siblings—would fall through. My memory is of spending many hours Christmas Eve night sitting at this opening waiting for Santa Claus to come. We would stay there until our mother would tell us, "Go to bed if you want Santa to come to our house," or until sleep overtook us. We would be so frustrated because we never could stay awake long enough to get a look at him.

This was also the place where we would wait for the Easter Bunny to come. But we never had any luck there either, because we never did get to see him.

The hole in the ceiling was also good for when we were banished to our bedroom for something we did or didn't do. Since the bedroom was on the second floor, we would sneak out of our room and sit at the hole in the ceiling and listen to everything going on downstairs. We had to be very quiet sitting there, because if Mom knew we were out of our room, she would yell, "Get back in your room!"

The stove in the living room was also just below this hole in the ceiling and would allow warmth to flow up into the sometimes very cold rooms upstairs.

Oh the joys of the hole in the ceiling!

Betty Ryan (nee Peddle)
Oromocto, New Brunswick

ಶ THE REGISTER ಶ

IN A RELATIVELY SMALL town like Grand Bank, I was sure everyone had the convenience of the hole in the kitchen ceiling. Now I find this wasn't always the case.

We referred to the hole as the "register." *Webster's Dictionary* describes the register as a perforated plate governing the opening into a duct, which admits warm air into a room for heat. If my memory serves me, our register was made of metal and measured approximately fourteen or sixteen inches square. A wheel rotated on either side to open or close it.

Our register was located in the bathroom, on the second floor, over the stove in the kitchen. As children we would wait for the stove to reach a good heat and then take turns dressing in the bathroom, as opposed to waiting for our cold bedrooms to warm up.

The kitchen was laid out such that there was a daybed in one corner between the wall and the stove. The register was located more or less above the daybed. On that daybed was where I did my reading of books like The Hardy Boys series and comic books.

I also remember my father taking a nap on the daybed after supper, after a hard day's work. Positioning myself over the register in the bathroom, with careful aim of my water pistol I could target my napping father's head. I think he knew the source because he would say, "Mother, go up and close the register."

While eavesdropping through the hole, we were privy to adult conversations. My dreams were shattered, though, when I heard my father telling my mother, "I have to keep Foster believing in Santa Claus by ringing the bells and shouting HO HO HO from the bottom of the stairs." That was even worse than when my friend opened the hatch in his house and dropped a sopping wet towel on his older sister and her boyfriend directly below. There's more than one way to have cold water thrown in your face.

Foster Thornhill
ST. JOHN'S

ཨ What Do You See? ཨ

Many of my memories of growing up on Empire Avenue in St. John's are very vivid. The hole was a source of precious little heat in the winter, as I recall ice forming on the inside windowsills of the bedroom.

I remember one particular day, when I was about five years old, my dear mother sent me upstairs to get her glasses that she had left by the bedside. She said she was blind without them. In my five-year-old mind the quicker I could get them to her the better. Subsequently, to carry out the task as quickly as possible, I decided to toss her glasses down to her via "the hole."

I remember bending over the hole, which was directly above the kitchen stove, reaching my arm down in it, glasses in hand, and swinging the glasses back and forth a few times. My five-year-old mind tried to calculate how much of a swing my arm would need to miss the stove and have the glasses land on the daybed (another creature comfort most homes don't have today).

My mother didn't look up until I called to her. Before she could get the word "DON'T!!" out of her mouth, the glasses were flung. My calculations were all wrong, and they smashed into smithereens on top of the stove.

I was scared to death and ran downstairs, crying, to find my mother sitting on the daybed speechless, with a strange, sad look on her face. I thought like any five-year-old would, "What have I done?" My mother was not only blind now but she couldn't talk either. She sat there for a very long time or what seemed like forever before she got up, wiped away my tears, and cleaned up the tiny shards of glass from the area. I can't remember how long it took for her to get new glasses, but the hole got covered that same day with some sort of lint-catching grate or wire mesh.

Another memory I have regarding the hole is directly connected to Saturday night bath time. This story was a dark secret for many years, as I was ashamed of my behaviour on that particular night.

As we were a large family, we often had to share the tub water that was dragged by the bucketful to the galvanized tub that sat in the middle of the kitchen floor. Bath time started with the younger ones, the older ones followed. One Saturday night—I can't exactly remember my age, let's just say it was the age of a prepubescent adolescent girl—I was lying in bed when I heard the splish-splash of one of my older brothers taking a bath. My resistance was low and my curiosity was high and the hole got the better of me. I crept out of bed ever so quietly, hoping neither the bedsprings nor the floorboards would squeak and give me away. Lying sideways on the floor I slithered closer and closer to the hole with my heart pounding louder than a sledgehammer and the closer to the hole I got, the louder it pounded. I was going to sneak a peek at a part of the male anatomy that we were not even permitted to acknowledge existed. I wasn't sure it really did.

After very cautiously positioning myself over the hole to get a clear view of my unsuspecting sibling, I was relieved to find nothing more than that my brother had a very hairy back for his age. My brother has since passed and I am confident he went to his grave never knowing he was betrayed by the hole and his younger sister.

Louise Fournier
BARRINGTON, NEW HAMPSHIRE

❦ On a String ❦

MY SISTER AND I shared a bedroom immediately above the kitchen stove when we were children. We lived in Bonavista. A hall stove provided minimal heat to the rest of the house, but the room over the kitchen was assigned to us because of its comfort level. This was due to the hole in the kitchen ceiling. The hole was covered by a grate mechanism that could be turned on and off by a lever on the side.

On Christmas Eve, however, it served a much more interesting and exciting raison d'être. We hung our stockings beside the kitchen stove in expectation of Santa's visit and the grate was removed. Our father used his imagination and creativity by tying strong string to our stockings, bringing it up through the hole, and tying it to our bedposts. On Christmas morning we untied the strings and pulled our filled stockings through the hole without having to leave the comfort of our beds. It is one of my most treasured childhood memories.

Beulah Inkpen
PORTUGAL COVE-ST. PHILLIP'S

Oops!

IN THE EARLY 1970S, my neighbour and I visited each other quite often, for tea and a chat. We both lived in Bonavista. She and her husband lived in a two-storey house, which had a hole in the kitchen ceiling. One night when I was visiting, her husband went to bed early because he had to go to work early in the morning. All of a sudden there was a crashing sound. What a fright!

It turned out that her husband heard us laughing so hard that he couldn't get to sleep. He threw the alarm clock across the bedroom's linoleum floor. It came crashing down through the hole onto the kitchen floor.

From then on, I visited my neighbour only when her husband was at work.

Beulah Morgan
CONCEPTION BAY SOUTH

The Hole Secret

When I was a lad living with my sisters in our ten-dollar-a-month Company house at West Mines Road, Bell Island, Conception Bay, Newfoundland, North America, the Whole Earth, the Milky Way, the Universe, my parents—even some adult neighbours—actually had a secret activity which they used effectively to control me, and I was too stunned to catch on.

They used that secret to put me on various pathways through my life, and I didn't know a thing about it until I was a full grown man with a young family of my own.

My parents and even outsiders exercised their secret control over me by use of a hole. It was a hole in the ceiling if you were downstairs, a hole in the floor if you were upstairs. Our hole, like all other such holes in the mining company's two-storey homes, was positioned in the middle of the four-by-four foot landing at the top of the stairs leading from the kitchen. That hole with its protective grate was right over the door frame separating the kitchen from the front room or parlour. Looking down through the hole, one could see into both rooms.

We called it "the heating hole" because it warmed the upstairs rooms during the winter days and nights when the downstairs kitchen and living room stoves were lit.

Oh how often I'd creep to that hole in the ceiling to spy on my mother and my father down below, especially if visitors were in, to hear what was being said, and observe their behaviour, like what they were being nice about, or why they were shouting.

Of the many times I secreted myself upstairs and made my observations, one afternoon stands out in my mind. It was a frosty winter day. Father came into the kitchen, removed the stove's two front dampers and the connecting centre piece, fitted some kindling into the wide open firebox, lit it with a match, and, going to the woodpile under the lid of the bench by the pantry, took out two long cloven junks, which he put on top of the roaring starter fire. As I was lying down on the floor at the top of the stairs, forehead, brows, and eyes just above the hole—being very careful not to let anyone know I was spying—the rush-rising of heat brought tears to my eyes and such a tickle to my throat I had to quickly snake back into my bedroom, no doubt red, if not green, in the face from the need to cough. With my head inside the quilts I smothered my hacking, and sneaked back to the hole when father turned on a spigot in a two-gallon heating-oil can near the living room stove just inside the kitchen door, got an immediate flare when he hauled a two-tone match across the prepared stiffness of the bum of his pants, and tossed the match into the belly of the stove. The heat from the two stoves soon became enough to kill ya. (That's the way people described being too hot; some would even say the heat was enough to kill ya dead, but I, long years away from getting out of school let alone becoming an editor, found no fault at all with that.)

"Mary!" he called to Mother, "is Ronnie IN or OUT?"

"I think he's OUT, Ike," she answered. "If not OUT, he's asleep in his room with the door closed. There's not been a squeak from up there for, oh, I dunno, maybe an hour or so."

Standing down there in the doorway, smack between the two stoves, Father said the Company nurse was giving needles to the children in Ronnie's school next week, and, "you know what?"

"What, Ike?"

"I'll bet you five cents that Ronnie will be one of the very, very few who won't cry when that needle is laid into his arm. Five cents, my maid!"

"I'll make it ten cents, Ike. Ronnie would never, ever cry over getting a needle. I never cried when I was a girl. Sure the needle is long, but it has such a tiny, tiny roundness to it that you can hardly even see it, let alone feel it."

"OK, Mary, I'll make it twelve cents he won't even screw up his face like some of the other boys will. He's a MAN, is Ronnie!"

The long and the short of it is, I took that needle, right here in my arm, look. Never even held my breath.

I later heard Father and Mother congratulate each other, right under the very hole I was looking down through, not daring to let them hear me breathe. "We both KNEW, knew damn well," said Father, "Ronnie wouldn't even flinch." And when Mrs. Providence Mercer came in from one of the two "next houses," my parents couldn't wait to tell her what a brave boy I'd been.

One day Mr. Walt Vokey, the foreman at the iron ore hoist across the way, was having a beer with my father, when my father called out to my mother, "Is Ronnie IN or OUT, Mary?" and mother promptly answered "OUT, Ike," whereupon I crept out of bed, slithered over to the hole, and cocked my ear in time to hear Father say, "Y'know, Ronnie is going to grow up without a broken back or a torn-off leg or a squashed head."

"Yeahhhh?" said Mr. Vokey. "Realllyyy Ike? Really?"

"Yes," said Father, raising his voice so Mother in the next room would hear him, "Ronnie is one smart boy. He looks up and down the street to see if any car or truck or even a bike is coming, BEFORE he makes a move to cross over."

"Really!" enthused Mr. Vokey. "Now, Ike, I wants to tell you, not many boys are as wise and smart as that Ronnie. Why, I know a father like yourself who used to beg his lad never ever to cross the street before looking both ways against a car or truck or bike knockin' him down and breakin' his back or crushin' his poor head. My, oh my, it is so good to know Ronnie is not like that."

Yes, and to this day, and I'm an old man now, I will not cross any street or even a laneway, without looking left and right.

Y'know I could go on, and tell you more about the secret that my dear parents knew, a secret they passed on to the neighbours, all of whom are dead now, but to all of whom I owe "many gratitudes."

The secret was this: Father or Mother ALWAYS knew when I was upstairs. When they wanted to teach their very stubborn Ronnie a lesson, being the smart people they were, they'd share between them their little code. I can hear it now, in my mind: "Is Ronnie IN or OUT?" When OUT was said loudly and clearly, it would relax me and set me up for their lesson, without their confronting me and having to beg, order, or threaten.

I was in my mid-fifties when, visiting the city of Cambridge,

Ontario, I heard that Mrs. Walt Vokey lived at such and such an address, her husband long deceased; I made a call on the ageing lady and shared a wonderful afternoon of memories with her.

It was then, only then, I learned of my parents' secret training routine.

To this very day I wonder about how very naïve I must have been in so many other ways.

Ron Pumphrey
ST. JOHN'S

CHAPTER 2

Lessons Learned

Making a splash

ಎ Lessons Learned ೬

My story about the hole in the ceiling could have ended in tragedy. It ended with no one getting hurt but one person in a lot of trouble, and a very valuable lesson was learned.

I grew up in Petty Harbour in my grandparents' house with my sister, my mother, and of course, my grandparents. Our house had a hole in the ceiling over the wood stove in the kitchen. Our bedroom was upstairs over the kitchen.

It was common practice for us to have a large boiler of water on the stove on Saturdays for everyone to bathe. My grandfather was quite feeble as a result of two strokes so we had a small place on the side of the stove set up for him to wash or shave.

My sister was two years old and I was seven. We had our bath and got in bed with Mom when she realized she had forgotten something. She told me to stay with my sister and that she would be right back. We always had a small mat over the hole and it made the room quite dark. When I realized this I became scared and jumped off the bed. My sister followed me, slipped on the mat, and fell right through the hole in the floor! She fell down on the boiler of water!

Thankfully, my grandfather was at the side of the stove shaving at the time. Although he was feeble, he was quick enough to catch her before she was hurt. We always loved watching the activities in the kitchen through the hole in the ceiling but things changed forever that night—the hole in the ceiling was no more.

Dolo Lee
St. John's

Submitted by Jacqueline Lee

❧ The Stove Between Them ❧

My grandfather, were he alive, would suggest that the hole in the kitchen ceiling had a far more personal and unique use for him—apart from it being a source of entertainment for the many Newfoundland children who would spy on adult company, when, indeed, these same children were supposed to be in bed.

The hole above the stove was used as a kind of chaperone for courting couples in Greenspond, Bonavista Bay. As every Newfoundlander of that generation would know, there were two seats, one on each side of the stove, known as a "settle." There was a gap—an open space, really—directly behind the oven where courting couples could look at each other and whisper together. Naturally, for propriety's sake, the distance between them was just enough so they could not hold hands. However, as my grandfather was from a strict United Church family, as was his fiancé, Emma, there had to be another protection for morality's sake.

When Pop called on Emma to court her, the kitchen emptied. Brothers, sisters, and parents traipsed up the stairs to the parents' bedroom, where all eyes and ears were focused on the courting couple. Imagine the nervous tension of two young people, knowing they were under such close supervision. As Pop said to me when he was in his ninety-sixth year. "'Tis a wonder, my maid, that you was ever born, considerin' how hard it was for me to court your Nan."

Jolene Gladney
Portugal Cove-St. Phillip's

ೲ The Whole Picture ೲ

NAN'S HOUSE IN ST. Anthony Bight was special. It had a special look, a special smell, and a special feel. It was different from any other "place" I had ever been. I don't know why it was so special; I just know that it was. It wasn't especially fancy. The furniture was well-worn and in need of repair; the floor, scantily covered by assorted bits of canvas, resembled a patchwork quilt; and the black and white photos on the walls could scare the devil himself, much less a nine-year-old plagued with an overactive imagination. It smelled of fresh bread, bleach, and Minard's Liniment. Nan liked to bake, had a thing about cleanliness, and had scores of ailments. It felt ordered and well contained, a place for everyone, and everyone and everything in its place. Nan's house had that something about it which made it memorable and distinct.

Pap was a fisherman. Everyone I knew had paps who were fishermen. I wondered, sometimes, what the other people did, the ones whose paps weren't fishermen. Sometimes I'd steal a peek of him over the top of my teacup and wonder what he would be if he weren't a fisherman. I couldn't see him as anything else. He always wore a navy Guernsey, bib overalls, and red-tapped rubbers turned down just right. His eyes, hidden behind horn-rimmed glasses, were always quiet and calm, and, sometimes, on the rare occasion that he laughed, they twinkled in a way which made you wish he'd do it more often. He always looked the same. I liked how he always looked the same.

Nan, her white hair curled to perfection with a Toni, would touch my hand—ever so slightly—that little secretive pat that told me not to stare. I didn't realize I was staring. I liked looking at Pap, how he pulled back his chair after a meal to have a smoke like it was dessert. I always thought maybe I was a little afraid of him, just because that's how respect presented itself. I'd never really been afraid, just openly fixated on the quiet man who told me so much without ever speaking.

37

People came and went at Nan's house. That's just how it was. The kitchen had a daybed covered with a hundred blankets and a fluffy pillow. There was a locker too; that's what Nan called it. It didn't look like a locker to me, not the kind we had at school. The wooden bench lined a full wall. It was topped with pillows that Nan had made from ratty clothes and old sheets. Underneath the locker's hinged top a treasure trove of trapped memorabilia triggered all kinds of crazy thoughts and created wonders for bored children longing to discover that extra special place where fairies and leprechauns played.

There was a hole in the kitchen ceiling, too. An honest-to-goodness hole that went up through the ceiling and into the blue room—the one that my father and my uncle had shared as children. The hole's practical purpose was to allow heat to rise to the second storey. But, I never quite understood the hole, and I never thought to ask. It was just another special thing that Nan's house had that ours didn't. I rather liked the hole, as silly as it seemed. Sometimes in the kitchen looking up I wondered if they watched us kids with Pap's binoculars to make sure we were sleeping. I didn't fancy the idea. When we turned in for the night, I put the grate over the hole because sleepy time was special, and I didn't care to share it.

We had fun with that old hole. In the summer, my cousins visited from Labrador. Oh, how Nan's house changed in those tangled-up days of no-school. I suppose we were quite the lot, three girls in all and my brother. We played goofy games, in the house and out, many of them centred around the hole. We were spy kids with our special perch high overhead. The grownups would forget the hole. They went about their business preoccupied, the way that grownups are—sputtering about what's for supper, who's bringing the water, whose turn to feed the dogs or make up the hay. We'd watch from the hole as they pitter-pattered about doing their errands. We'd laugh at them, too, especially on washday when Nan hung her bloomers on the hook behind the stove to dry. Then we'd watch her scrabble when someone came home. Sometimes, she wore bloomers on her head when she was baking. She didn't scrabble then. As soon as those bloomers had a practical use, it was OK to wear them on her head.

My brother was a case—like the time he found a gull's long tail feather on the beach—the kind Nan used in the inkwell to write letters to Uncle Sid, who lived away—and he stole a long piece of rope from the twine loft where Pap mended the nets.

"Watch this," he said, as young fingers, already trained to tie those weird fishermen's knots, fastened the feather to the string.

My cousin was the decoy. We sent her downstairs bawling, that she had a bad belly. Nan, with her catlike grace, and pantyhosed feet, wrinkled thick around her ankles, wasted no time. She sputtered to her room to get her Andrew's Liver Salts that she kept in a special container in her trunk by the bed. With the kitchen empty now, Pap, napping on the locker, was fair game. We all held our breath as my brother lowered the feather to Pap's sleeping form. Well, we had never seen anything so funny. We carefully tickled Pap's face and hands. He never woke up, but he made all kinds of silly sounds and movements, as he attempted to bat the feather away. Then my bawling cousin ran in, and Nan was on her way back to the kitchen. There was some kind of suspense then, getting that feather back into the blue room on time.

Nan baked lots. The odour of cinnamon, apples, and molasses buns drifted up through that hole more often than I can remember. It made our stomachs growl, and our mouths water something fierce. It required some thought, but we mastered a plan to get those buns while they were still hot. Again, my brother was the brains of the operation—I don't know if he was really the brains, or that he just knew his way around the stores and the stage. A four-pronged jigger was the solution to the bun-fetching puzzle. Bun-fetching required two people downstairs, one to occupy Nan, and the other to stab the buns onto the jigger. Now Nan wasn't easily distracted. Many great performances went unnoticed. When finally we hit the showstopper, one of us would motion my brother to drop the jigger. Like a big, old juggernaut cast out of heaven, the jigger was lowered through the hole. Quick fingers stabbed the lassy buns, and a steady hand raised the treats carefully into the blue room. We had some feeds in that room, careful of the crumbs which would tattle on us all.

Sometimes, there was a crowd at Nan's house. I used to wonder who all those people were and how each had a role to play in our little-outport lives. I was somewhat shy and all those people, talking, laughing, singing, and smoking … well, they were a bit scary. They drank tea mostly and sometimes dogberry wine. One guy always brought his accordion and another his mouth organ—I never did remember their names. They croaked out tuneless songs as they jumped around the kitchen, stamping their feet and wiggling about like their bums were on fire. I don't think they knew how crazy they looked.

There were other times when I wished the hole wasn't there, or, at least, that I had had the sense to leave the blue room when I should have. I remember the sun and how it filtered the dust-filled air the day my aunt told Nan that her brother had drowned. I thought the sun so disrespectful, when below me there was such grief. I'd never seen grief before, having been sheltered from all things bad and ugly. How Nan cried. How I wished that she would stop. My heart hurt, my eyes stung, my body ached; everything was no longer ordered and perfect. I covered up the hole with the grate and then threw a blanket over it. I told Patrick I didn't like the hole. Patrick knew everything about me, because I hugged him close every night, and he knew all my dreams. He was very understanding, for a bear.

For a long time afterwards, I didn't like the hole. I kept it covered and no one seemed to notice. Sometimes, grownups don't notice. They didn't notice the covered hole, or the coldness upstairs, or that not every child played like the others. Then, one day, Nan came into the blue room and she took away the blanket and the grate. The heat rose quickly. She came close and patted Patrick's head. She smiled then, and I smiled too.

My cousins, my brother, and I had all kinds of mysteries. Like how sundogs could tell the weather, where snowbirds went in summer, and how Uncle Bill had been fairy-led one summer when the fog made him senseless. The greatest mystery ever was how Pap got so many bakeapples—even summers when they didn't grow thick, Pap always got his bucket full. We knew well berry-picking days. They were days in August when it was too rough to go fishing. We'd hightail it to the blue room as soon as Pap started looking for his bucket. Surely, he'd tell Nan where he was going, because he could take sick, or something could happen. How we listened, how we tried to read more into his actions, how we wanted to go with him, how we wanted to follow. A goat, he was. He meandered over those rocks with the speed of an Acadian motor. We couldn't keep up. He must have heard us rustling in the trees, but he never let on. He never slowed down, and he never mentioned it later. Like any good mystery, it remained unsolved.

I can't forget "kissy times." Well, they were the best fun of all. The sight of adults kissing ... I suppose, that's enough said. I used to wonder if, when I grew up, I would ever want to be part of such foolishness. Boys were so gross, but my aunts, uncles, older cousins, and people who came to visit, well, they all eventually took turns at this kissing business. It was just so funny, how their lips puckered like sculpins, how they got all flustered, how they started talking gibberish. We'd laugh so hard that our stomachs got sore, and we'd have to cover our mouths with pillows. One time my cousin threw up—that made us laugh even more. Sometimes the kissing people would hear us, and they'd throw a boot or something up through the hole to drive us away.

Nan's house is still standing. The hole is still there. There is nothing to look down upon these days, just memories. The man with the accordion and the man with the mouth organ are gone; there are no more dancers. Nan is gone. Pap is gone. My cousins no longer visit. Below me, there is no locker, no daybed. The stove's still there, but it doesn't work; no more hot air to rise. The grate's in place. I lift it back, as I remember Nan. I never did find all of Pap's special berry-picking spots. I know I wasn't meant to. I think of them all the time on those little footpaths that reach nowhere—where the present forever meets the past, and reaches for the future.

I feel a silent whisper. It's the corn tree outside, untamed and wild now, scratching on the kitchen window. There's a draft. It reaches past the rotting timbers, across the abandoned kitchen, and up through the hole. I am right where I belong.

A hole, by definition, is a "hollow space." Funny, how this hollow space contains so much of everything.

Sherry Pilgrim-Simms
St. Anthony Bight

The Hooked Mat

When I thought about the hole in the kitchen ceiling after so many years, I had a great laugh. I could see my sister and me in bed in a duplex on St. Clare Avenue in St. John's. In 1939, I was about eight years old, but I am eighty now. My sister is now seventy-eight. Our bedroom was next to Mom and Dad's. Their room was directly over the kitchen stove and the hole in the kitchen ceiling had a hooked mat over it.

One night my sister woke up and crept into our parents' room to get in bed with them. She stepped on the mat and went straight down the hole.

She hit the stove, dented the kettle and never got a scratch. They said the mat broke her fall all the way.

Today my sister is a granny and great-granny who survived the kitchen ceiling hole. Thank God that through the years, life has become so much easier and warmer.

Unsigned
St. John's

❧ The Hockey Game ☙

I have many fond memories of the hole in the upstairs landing. Ours was a series of small circular holes cut in the floor above the kitchen. I lived with my grandparents in St. Anthony on the Northern Peninsula. They were well known probably because my grandfather was the mail carrier between St. Anthony and outlying communities and also because they were a hospitable, caring couple. Frequently people from outside communities who came to St. Anthony for medical treatment or childbirth would stay in our home for extended periods.

I remember vividly one Christmas Eve when I was supposed to be asleep, I heard excitement and laughter from downstairs. When I crept to the peep holes in the hall floor, I could see my grandfather and one of our guests playing a hockey game (the kind where a marble was the puck and rods at either end would move the players). I knew it had to be mine! I dared not say a word until Christmas Day when I became its rightful owner.

There were numerous other nights when I just couldn't fall asleep, so I would interest myself in the adult conversations, as my grandparents and friends enjoyed a good lunch together. What wonderful memories!

Rex Colbourne
NORTHERN ARM

૱ The Hatch ༀ

Dedicated to my sister Bon

"Open the hatch, it's freezing up here, we can see our breath!"—a common phrase heard almost as often as the pump cutting in every time we flushed the toilet in our house in Martin's Lane, Torbay.

I'll always remember that old hatch, as we called it. The hatch was the cover for the hole, the hole that was right above Nanny's pot-bellied wood stove. It was the only source of heating the entire upstairs. Who crawls into a bed anymore with twenty or thirty pounds of blankets and mismatched quilts, heavy with flour sacks and Nanny's old drawers? The bed would be icy cold for about two minutes and then we would be ready for the coziest sleep ever. Right before, you'd hear our mother or father bawling out, "Say your prayers, I'm turning off the light! Sleep tight!"

We were never allowed to hang out with the adults, especially when guests dropped by. Every time someone visited, it was always through the kitchen. Everything happened in the kitchen. We had the best seating possible from above. That Kleenex-box-size little hole in the ceiling was like the best balcony seating at some fancy opera. Sometimes that little hatch felt like a window to the world, a prime spot for eavesdropping on the adults. The hatch was our window to the adult world! And, yes, for playing pranks on our brothers and sisters too.

The hole wasn't really big enough for two little faces to look through, let alone three little faces. We fought with each other—if one took longer than the other looking down the hatch—we took turns at pulling the hair of the sister or brother who hogged the hole. We couldn't bear the heat for long, either, it was so intense. The hatch was directly above the damper of the wood stove. Our little faces got beet red from the heat. At times we'd spit down through the hole, to hear our saliva sizzle on the scalding hot stove. Then we'd hear shouts from our mother: "Don't be so saucy!," "Stop that!," "Where did ye learn that?," or "I'll go up there and give ye a crack yet." And we'd laugh at the sizzling spit as it danced on the stove.

In the spring, we'd gather the carpenters when those little crispy-backed bugs paraded around the house and we gathered them up in an old glass bottle, their little legs wiggling as we turned them upside down so they wouldn't escape. And then we'd drop them on the hot stove—down through that hole in the ceiling. I remember the awful smell of burnt carpenters, or sow bugs as they are called now. What a stink! Pop would say, "Them youngsters are at it again! Maggie, get the broom and clean off the stove!" And we'd still giggle.

Funnier times occurred when relatives from away came to visit or neighbours dropped by at Christmastime. They were such important dignitaries, at those times children were "seen and not heard." They wouldn't pull out the accordion, they'd pull my sister out of her bed—like she was attached to the accordion—because she was the lucky one who carried on the tradition of accordion playing handed down from Nanny. It was more of a demand and, always reluctantly, she'd give in. What choice did she have? Shy as my sister was to these strangers, their insistence meant she had permission to hang out with the adults. And it was the only time. If I played something, I would have been down with them too, and probably allowed to have a glass of Coke or ginger ale or real Purity syrup (with more water than syrup, as only the guests would get), as they drank and laughed and sang and enjoyed my sister's talent with the accordion.

They danced around the youngster playing the accordion in such frenzy that they'd be stomping and kicking up their heels. We'd feel the house vibrating, and she'd have to play song after song—fast and slow ones, "Up the Pond" or "Mussels in the Corner" or anything else they wanted. Then you'd hear the roars as my sister belted out the tunes.

"Woo hoo!"

"Get up in yer stall!"

She would be made to play that accordion and she did quite well at it, but we'd be upstairs looking down through that hatch, our hot little faces poking fun at her for having to play. We would be poking our fingers at her and giggling, making her feel more shy and nervous. The guests would continue to dance around her and she would be playing into the wee hours of the morning until the moonshine or Screech or Old Sam ran out.

We were full of devilment, like little puppies. I suppose we were just trying to mock my sister for having to endure such daunting tasks or perhaps we were just plain jealous.

I miss that old hatch. I'm sure it's still there under the carpet. It would be a piece of art now if you could cut out that piece of the floor and frame it.

Paul Martin
Toronto, Ontario

Submitted by Barbara Thorne

❧ Blueberry Muffins and Raisin Buns ❧

OH MY! THE HOLE in the ceiling! We enjoyed many an evening peering down through the grate, watching the grown-ups. And you had to be careful not to let the dust float down on someone's head, and get caught!

Not only did we get to listen to conversations not meant for our ears, but the smell of the treats Mom put out for company was something to treasure. Smelling the food wasn't enough for us. I wasn't the youngest of eight children, but certainly the smallest. One night my brothers decided that we could sneak some blueberry muffins or raisin buns out of the kitchen while our parents and friends were in the "front room" (now known as the "living room"). In order to pull off this feat without getting caught, they came up with the idea to lower me through the hole and have me pilfer the goods. Well, I did fit, just barely, and they were able to get me down no problem. I scurried across the room and grabbed the raisin buns, like the little mouse I was. Hauling me back up wasn't as easy for the boys, but they managed, with a lot of laughing, and we got away with the scheme.

A more personal favourite memory I have is one of laying my head on the open grate, enjoying the rising heat and watching Mom read her book. I felt so safe and peaceful and drifted off to sleep there on the floor. I think this is where I got my passion for reading. Thank you, Mom.

The kitchen in that house on Blackmarsh Road, St. John's, has been renovated, and the hole closed up. The old grate hung around for a while, but was eventually discarded.

Maureen Ryan
MOUNT PEARL

Uncle Doff Goes to the East Indies

SO MANY CHILDHOOD MEMORIES collide at the mere mention of that unique feature of a hole in the kitchen ceiling. It was known as "the shutter" in my home in Springdale. You see, that hole was so much more than just a hole. Not only did it provide warmth in an era before central heating, it was also a lens through which to view the rural Newfoundland and Labrador that existed fifty years ago.

It was used to talk to Mom in the kitchen below about when meals were ready, when it was warm enough to come down to the kitchen to finish dressing for school, or to get advice on what to wear to go "down the road." Most importantly, it allowed me to hear the stories my father and his friends shared in the gifted narrative of true Newfoundland storytellers. They could spin a yarn for an hour over something as simple as a cobweb, especially with a glass of Screech on the table. These yarns usually took place on Sunday evening when Mom went to church, leaving Dad in charge of my younger sister and me.

My favourite memory took place on one of those Sunday evenings. Not five minutes after Mom had left for church, Dad's seafaring friend Uncle Doff knocked and came through the kitchen door. We were gently reminded of bedtime, taking that as our hint to leave the adults to their time alone in the kitchen. My sister and I went willingly, knowing that our room had the shutter and we would hear some of the best bedtime stories ever!

Getting ready for bed on those evenings took all of two minutes, so we wouldn't miss anything. With our pajamas on, my sister and I took our pillows over to the shutter and lay down prepared to be quiet as church mice. We knew that if we made a sound the shutter would be closed and we would miss out on the yarn being told in the kitchen below.

Sure enough, we went out the kitchen door and Dad brought out the glasses for just a drop for Uncle Doff and him. That night Uncle Doff told the story of his first trip to the East Indies, now known as the Caribbean. You see, he was a sailor on a schooner that did the salt fish/

rum trade that delivered salt fish to those faraway places and brought home rum, the kind sitting on our kitchen table that night.

Dad was an adventurer at heart, who never had the opportunity to travel, so when Uncle Doff came to visit, he was as enthralled as we were listening from the shutter. That night Uncle Doff told about when he'd sailed out of the cold and wet here at home to arrive at a place so totally unbelievable to us. He talked of the endless sun and blue sky and how it was so hot even in the middle of winter. We were there with him to see how the local people could swim like fish and dive forever, without a breath, in water as warm as a bath. We saw the lush tropical island, the people wearing brilliant colours and balancing baskets on their heads. We heard them talking and singing in a foreign language which didn't need any translation! He made it all come alive in the way of a true storyteller!

We didn't make a peep for an hour. We knew Mom would soon be home when Uncle Doff put his glass in the sink without a word and told Dad he'd see him next time. Sure enough, Mom would arrive home within the few minutes it took Dad to put away the bottle, pick up his *National Geographic* and for us to sneak quietly into bed. We don't know to this day if Mom knew about those visits. We were smart enough as kids not to ask.

As an adult those images created by Uncle Doff came to life as I travelled to those same sun destinations. Those childhood images became a dream realized as I vacationed in the Caribbean. That story heard through the hole in the kitchen ceiling so long ago was lived out in a reality that even now competes with that long-ago memory.

JoAnna Bennett
PARADISE

❧ The Kitchen ☙

The kitchen in the house where I grew up had two holes in the ceiling: we had heat in two bedrooms. There were three doors in the kitchen—the porch door, the hall door, and the pantry door. Usually each kitchen had two windows—one at the end and one at the front so as to get the sun at all times.

In some houses the woodbox and the split box were in the kitchen, while in other houses they were on the porch. In our house in Plate Cove East, Bonavista Bay, the chimney was in the kitchen. A wood stove was connected by a funnel to the chimney. On the stove were two kettles, one iron one and one nickel. The nickel kettle was used to boil water for tea or cocoa, ginger wine, or peppermint.

There was also a couch called a settle or bench in the kitchen. Over the stove was a wooden pole suspended from the ceiling by a wire; clothes were hung there to dry. If the man of the house used a long razor, a leather belt called a razor strop was hung by the chimney to hone the razor.

A bracket attached to the wall held the kitchen lamp. The bedroom lamps were laid on a shelf, which was attached to one wall.

There was also a cabinet for dishes, called a dresser. In some houses there were two kitchens—a back kitchen and a front kitchen.

Geraldine Keough
Bonavista Bay

❧ No Holes Barred ❧

With his slick black hair and chiselled features, Uncle Bill was the Clark Gable of his day. His mad pursuit of lovely ladies was as legendary as his appetite for homemade bread, pies, and cookies. So it was his extreme good taste to romance Bess, the daughter of the acclaimed Mrs. Baker, famous for her molasses buns.

Shortly after the courtship began, Uncle Bill was invited in for tea and buns following the Saturday night dance at the parish hall in Whitbourne. Bess was so delighted that she forgot to tell Uncle Bill that her mother went to bed early and didn't want to keep the fire going after ten-thirty.

Around midnight Uncle Bill remembered the treat awaiting him and rushed Bess toward the door.

"Wait," said Bess, "I just remembered that my parents are in bed now and we'll have to go another time. Mom bakes every Saturday."

"Surely you can pour me a cup of tea and pass me a bun, can't you?" he said, while stuffing her into her coat and boots.

"The fire is out now," said Bess.

But he was determined and whisked her out the door, into his Model T.

The moon looked like a silver seal on grey parchment and a few unruly clouds dimmed the moonlight as they raced over the hills of Burnt Cove toward the lamplight flickering in Mrs. Baker's kitchen window. Undaunted, Uncle Bill with Bess in tow brazened his way up to the door.

Abruptly, the door swung out knocking off Uncle Bill's sealskin hat.

"Get in here, the two of you. Waiting all night I was, keeping the kettle on and the buns warm. I allow they're all dried up now and I even put in the last of the raisins," said Mrs. Baker, clouting her daughter with a bleached dishtowel.

Without a word they sat at the table laid out with her best china sparkling on the linen sent from Ireland. She snatched up her best teapot trimmed with gilt and flung a handful of dried tea leaves into the belly and poured what was left of the scalding water into the pot. Suddenly she planked a pyramid of brown buns pierced with raisins directly in front of Uncle Bill.

Without hesitation he took several buns, buttered them as if he were liming a fence and gobbled them like a gannet in herring season. Bess picked out the raisins and ate them while stirring her tea in an attempt to drown out her escort's lip-smacking appreciation of her mother's treat.

At last the mother went to bed, but not without warning Uncle Bill to hurry up.

However, he continued to stuff himself and relished the idea of having Bess all alone, until, as if from on high, a voice interrupted his plans.

"Is that young man gone yet?" asked her mother from the hole above the kitchen stove.

"Not yet," Bess replied.

Never to be denied, Uncle Bill coaxed Bess to say "yes" the next time she asked.

Soon came the same question to which Bess assured her mother that, indeed, he was gone.

"Well, he is one son of a bitch to eat buns," said her mother.

Angela Otto
St. John's

This story was contributed by one of the judges, but was excluded from the judging process.

The Sleepwalker

When I was about ten or eleven years old (I'm almost seventy-two), I had a little sleepwalking experience, or so I'm told: My older sister and I were in bed asleep in our upstairs bedroom at our family home in Charlottetown, Bonavista Bay. The hole in the kitchen ceiling was at the foot of our bed. I must have been dreaming and got out of bed at the foot. At this young age I was as skinny as a rake, and when I stepped off the end of the bed I stepped right into the hole and went straight down into the kitchen. I even broke the clothesline that Mom had strung across the kitchen to dry the baby clothes and didn't wake up. I did wake up when my head touched the top of the cold kitchen stove. After this little mishap, my mother made sure the hole got covered every night at bedtime.

Ethel Chaulk
CHARLOTTETOWN

Making Popcorn

as prepared by Victor R. Pittman, Shoal Harbour

AH, THE MEMORIES OF the hole in the ceiling!

I grew up in a big house in Harcourt, Trinity Bay, in the days when central heating was unheard of. Our only source of heat was the big cast iron Waterloo stove in the kitchen and, of course, the hole in the ceiling provided some heat to the bedroom above. So, needless to say, during cold weather we never spent much time anywhere other than in these two rooms.

In summertime the reverse was true, because the stove had to be used to do the cooking, to heat water for laundry and our baths, and for ironing. So the bedroom with the hole was not so popular in the summer.

I can remember when I was a little girl I didn't like the dark (of course we had no electricity) and I loved to sleep in the bedroom with the hole. It was so comforting to be snuggled in my featherbed with the gleam of light and the murmur of voices coming from the kitchen. It made me feel cozy and safe as I drifted off to sleep.

Some memories of the hole have little to do with the reason it was there. When I married, we lived in my husband's family home, which also had a hole in the ceiling. One winter, his brother with his wife and their young son, who had never been to Newfoundland before, came to visit from Toronto. Naturally they were given the warm room with the hole.

Early next morning, Johnny was anxious to get up but his parents kept telling him it was too early, saying, "Your aunt and uncle aren't up yet."

But Johnny looked down the hole and said excitedly, "Yes Mommy, they're up and making popcorn."

What he thought was corn popping was the fire crackling in the wood stove.

Another time we had relatives visiting with their little three-year-old girl. While we sat chatting over our tea after our meal, the little one wandered upstairs. All at once we heard her screaming and her father rushed into the living room to find her on top of the bookcase. He scolded her for climbing up there only to find out that she had just landed there on her way down after falling through the hole in the ceiling. Luckily she wasn't hurt and we forgot about it until bedtime.

When her mother went to put her to bed, the little girl stood at the bottom of the stairs and said, "Mommy, I'm not going up there because I nearly broke my neck up there." Then we could laugh about it even though it had given us quite a scare.

Minnie Goodyear
CLARENVILLE

❧ The Powers through the Ages ☙

We lived in Branch, St. Mary's Bay, in one of the oldest houses, a traditional two-storey clapboard structure that is an indigenous form of Newfoundland architecture. It was built at the latest in 1896 and its date of construction might even precede that date, since outport fishermen often had their houses built for years before being able to afford to marry. It has housed four generations of our family and continues to be a family home to a present generation of Powers.

Our house boasted a traditional hole, even two. There was one in the kitchen ceiling, which connected directly with Nanny's bedroom, and another in the dining room indicating a time when that room served as a kitchen before certain renovations were made.

The purpose of the hole—in our case a small round opening about the size of an egg cup—was to heat the bedrooms on the second floor. Like all outport homes, ours had a single source of heat, the stove in the kitchen. For the children, however, the hole in the kitchen ceiling was of dubious value.

The family kitchen could be a noisy place, with neighbours gathering to listen to the radio and children sitting at the table in the only warm room in the house to do homework. Nanny—old even when we were all young—usually went to bed early and the constant hubbub in the kitchen often prevented her getting to sleep at a reasonable hour. Because of the hole, all noise ascended to her room. She was not remiss when it came to reminding us that the noise was disrupting her sleep. She was particularly disturbed by music, and it seemed that our favourite Friday night radio program of Irish music, brought to us courtesy of The Big Six, once a number, now an institution, was "no music" to her ears. I remember my mother on many occasions cautioning us about the noise level just by pointing up to the hole, which was a clear reminder that Nanny was in easy listening range. We never had access to the hole upstairs since Nanny's room was off limits to all.

There was also a hole in the dining room, which at one time used to be the kitchen. There was less to be seen there, since the dining room was not the centre of the house as was the kitchen. One of the favourite occupations of my brothers—the boys' room was directly above this hole—was to annoy those downstairs by constantly throwing objects down through the hole to land on the dining room table. There were frequent threats of what Mom would do if she was forced to march upstairs to deal with the miscreants.

We wonder now how we survived winters in our Newfoundland homes without central heating. Maybe our lack of creature comforts accounts for the traditional hardiness of Newfoundlanders. Like so many other vestiges of outport living the heating holes are now a thing of the past.

I had not thought of them for a long time when one day a few years ago while visiting my old home I noticed there was no longer an opening all the way through. Bedrooms now are carpeted and the holes have disappeared. There is electric heat in all the rooms upstairs, so the traditional holes will no longer be part of the architecture of outport homes. Present-day children will never find a listening post as good as the ceiling holes often provided for so many older generations!

Celine Power Kear
WINNIPEG, MANITOBA

❧ Properly Set ❧

I don't have much memory of the hole because we moved from our old two-storey house when I was seven and our new house was a bungalow. Both were in South Branch, in the Codroy Valley. But I can remember when I was very small, looking down and seeing my parents sitting at the table eating lunch before going to bed. Mom always set the table even if it was only for a lunch. There was always a tablecloth and in those days, no mugs but cups and saucers, with a small plate for the bread, and a knife and a spoon. We don't have such ceremony anymore.

Sometimes there would be people there, mostly men, at what I suppose was a party. I would watch and listen through the hole but I couldn't understand much of what was said. However, it would entertain me until I got sleepy and went back to bed—where everyone thought I was anyway.

Barbara Brennan
St. John's

❦ Caught in the Act ❧

as told by Hannah McDonald

IN THE 1960S MY mother and father rented a house in Mount Carmel, Salmonier. It was a lumbering two-storey with four bedrooms, and a huge back room off one of the bedrooms. Given that we were a family of four, a small family in those times, there was plenty of space in our home for company. And company Mom and Dad often had. Mom's nephews, Bob and Bill from St. John's were regulars. Many a summer vacation they spent in Mount Carmel, a children's paradise. There was swimming in the ocean, catching pricklies in the brook, playing cowboys and Indians in the woods, riding in Uncle Jerry's dump truck, helping Aunt Hannah with her chickens, and a myriad of other experiences that brought delight to these city boys. For the most part they spent all of their time outdoors playing and having fun. That is, of course, unless it was a day with heavy rain.

The rains had started in the morning and continued on during the day. The boys had been playing and roughhousing for most of the morning, but were starting to get on each other's nerves. Mom was upstairs in one of the bedrooms pushing the dry mop under the bed. She could hear the boys squabbling downstairs in the kitchen. As the sounds escalated Mom went to the hole in the floor to observe their shenanigans.

As she stared down at them, she both heard and saw the slap; then Bob yelled, "Aunt Hannah, Aunt Hannah, make Bill stop, he's hitting me!"

Bill shouted, "I'm not touching him Aunt Hannah; he's lying."

Then Mom's voice came down from above, "Well, I must be blind then!"

Poor Bill flipped his head back and looked up to see Mom peering through the hole, and knew then he had been caught in the act.

Agatha McDonald
SALMONIER

CHAPTER 3

Buttons, Buttons ... I Found the Buttons

Trouble with buttons

Buttons, Buttons ...
❧ I Found the Buttons ☙

as told by Mary Cooney

"**Aunt Lucy and Uncle** Ned want to talk to Father and me alone for a little while. It would help if you girls would tell the little ones some stories until they fall asleep," said Mother one night. Surprised, but eager to please, Lucy, Ella, and I scrambled up the stairs to the younger girls' room, where Margaret and Gertie were tucked in their bed. On the other side of the room, Angeline was sitting up in the cozy wooden cot Father had made before our oldest sister Josephine was born. Tears rolled down Angeline's cheeks as she cried, "M...M... Mom."

While Lucy and Ella lay with the others, telling them the same stories over and over, I comforted Angeline. We sat in Mother's big homemade rocker, snuggled under a patchwork quilt. Angeline cuddled into me as I sang a song Mother had sung to me as a baby:

Hush little baby don't say a word
Momma's gonna buy you a mocking bird
If that mocking bird don't sing
Momma's gonna buy you a diamond ring

As her eyes finally closed and her woolly toy lamb fell to the floor, I gently lifted her back to her crib. Margaret and Gertie were already drifting off to sleep. We older girls were free to find out what all the secrecy was about downstairs.

Quiet as mice, Lucy, Ella, and I crept to the hall stairs to sit one behind the other, as we often did when Mother and Father had company. Lifting the lace curtains, my sisters and I peeked through the window of the parlour door to the kitchen.

Father and Aunt Lucy sat on the daybed with their heads close together. With Kissie their puppy sitting on his lap, Uncle Ned with brown-stained fingers tapped Target tobacco into his pipe. Mother rocked quietly in her chair with her hands under her white starched apron. Her brow was knit together as tightly as the double braid around her head. She only loosened her hair, which had never been cut, before she went to bed. It fell around her shoulders as she liberally sprinkled Holy Water over us, while we pretended to be asleep.

Leaning closer to the railing, we could hear the murmur of voices.

"Will," Aunt Lucy said, "you know me and Neddie would love for one of your girls to come live with us as our own."

"What?" whispered Lucy, hitting me on the shoulder so hard I almost went headlong into Ella. "What did she say?"

Ella looked from Lucy to me as I said, "Hush! Listen!"

Rubbing his forehead, Father gave a long sigh. Mother stopped rocking. She looked at Aunt Lucy and said, "Not one of my children will leave this house unless she wants to."

"Well, Maggie, I thought we would be helping one another out. She could come to Labrador with us in the summer and go to school in the fall. Neddie and I can afford to educate a child and give her a good home."

I held my breath. My knees were shaking. Was Aunt Lucy talking about us?

"Not me!" said Lucy, as she popped up and down on the stairs. I'm staying right here with Mother. Aunt Lucy always says I have to control my temper, but she's the one who makes me mad."

"If you keep talking, they will hear us," I whispered, "and none of us will go." Ella, only five years old, looked ready to cry. I leaned towards the stairwell, straining to hear what the adults would say next.

"Any of the other children could come to our house whenever they want. We would visit Neddie's family in Philadelphia during Christmas and even Kissie would enjoy the girls' company," continued Aunt Lucy.

Uncle Ned cleared his throat and said, "Our house needs young people, Maggie, and we'd be honoured to have one of yours."

Father reached towards Mother, patting her hand gently as he said, "What do you think, Maggie?"

Mother didn't say anything for a long time. They all waited. Aunt Lucy and Uncle Ned looked towards Mother. She took her handkerchief from her pocket, wiped her eyes and crushed it between her fingers. Slowly, she put the handkerchief back in her pocket.

Ella and I squeezed one another while Lucy nearly fell on us to hear what Mother would say.

Sitting very straight, looking from Father to Aunt Lucy and Uncle Ned, Mother finally said, "We have always kept our children together, even when Will was laid up with his leg. Every one of them is a masterpiece and, to us, each one is very special."

"Yes," said Father, "a better lot of children you will never find. Jim and Pad got work at the mines in Buchans this winter. John and Duncan, two clever lads, are working in the woods with me." Father paused as he looked at Mother, who having removed a pair of treasured rosary beads from her pocket was now slipping them through her fingers.

In a low voice we could barely hear, she said, "As you know, Josephine, our oldest girl, has settled in Philadelphia. Annie has to rest so she can recover from TB. Lucy, who is almost nine, helps take care of the little ones. Since Angeline was born last fall, Margaret and Gertie cling to me more than ever. They were difficult to settle, even tonight. After all, they are only two and four years old." Mother paused and took a deep breath. "About the only ones who could go are Mary or Ella," she finally said. "I know they love to visit you and Lucy for a few hours but I'm not sure if they would even stay overnight."

Ella's eyes were as round as saucers as she reached for my hand. The more I heard, the more my head was spinning. Aunt Lucy and Uncle Ned lived in South River, about a half-hour carriage ride from our house. Since my seventh birthday in the fall, I was allowed to visit by myself as a special treat.

While at their house, I explored bags of delicate seashells collected on faraway beaches.

A glass of goat's milk and Aunt Lucy's crunchy gingerbread men were often set out for my lunch on a little table by the bookshelf. I liked to browse the musty old photo albums trying to figure out who those people were with the funny-looking clothes. Aunt Lucy said the next time I visited she would show me her special treasure trunk which she kept in her bedroom. I felt so lucky. Ella and Lucy could hardly believe it when I told them. Although we had visited many times, Aunt Lucy had never allowed us to play in her bedroom and, in fact, we had never even been in that room.

Ella, poking me in the ribs, said, "I think Father saw us."

Father rose as he spoke, "Whatever you think, Maggie, is fine with me. We love all our children and only want what is best for them."

"I feel so selfish, Will, when I think this may be a real opportunity for one of the girls," said Mother.

Father cleared his throat, glanced towards the window of the door, confirming Ella's suspicion and beckoned us into the kitchen.

As we filed in, Mother pulled Lucy and me to her. Father held out his arms to Ella, who jumped up, holding on to his neck. "Were you snooping on us, girls?" he asked, as he winked at Mother. We didn't say anything. "Well, never mind. You've heard what Aunt Lucy and Uncle Ned had to say. Tell us what you think of it," he said, as he sat back on the daybed by Aunt Lucy, still holding Ella.

Glancing at my sisters, but before they could say a word, I said, "Father, I would like to go with them."

Aunt Lucy got up quickly, kissed me on the cheek and said, "I knew Mary wouldn't turn me down. No flies on her, Maggie, to make up her mind."

Mother got up as she wiped her eyes with her apron. She paused, held out her arms to hug me tightly before she said, "You can try it for a little while, Mary, to see what you think. Father and I will go with you to their house tomorrow. You can stay until next Sunday after Mass, when you, Aunt Lucy, and Uncle Ned will come back to our house for dinner."

Father sniffed loudly, patted me on the head and said, "Now everyone off to bed before the sandman comes."

Lucy and Ella hooked their fingers into mine, squeezing my hands tightly as we scooted off to bed.

*

Early morning, Aunt Lucy liked to hang out the clothes that she washed the night before. I would have helped her, but I didn't know yet how to sort the darks and lights as she liked. Slowly she would teach me her way of doing things around the house.

"That's OK, Mary, you can set the table for dinner a little later this morning. Our good friends the Pikes from Harbour Grace will be here, and I invited Monsignor Dinn to join us. I would like them to meet the newest member of our family," she smiled.

With the sun already melting the snow, Uncle Ned was in the shed mending nets for the spring fishery in Labrador. He, Aunt Lucy and a crew of ten men went to Labrador on the coastal boat, the *Kyle*, each year. The *Kyle* transported Newfoundlanders from Conception Bay and other ports to places like Black Tickle on the Labrador Coast. Aunt Lucy had already told me, "When we get there, you and I will take a punt to explore the islands, looking for the ripest bakeapples. But before we leave, I will take you to Ralph's store in Clarke's Beach for rain boots, jacket, and Cape Ann to be ready for adventure in all weather." I could hardly wait.

Looking out the window of the sitting room I could see lots of mud puddles in the lane to try out new boots now if I had them. Even without boots, if Lucy and Ella were here with me we could play hopscotch, marbles, and skipping rope. Maybe they were feeding the baby chicks this morning or helping Mother spread Father's work clothes on the fence. "Did they miss me?" I wondered. Only my stomach answered with little growls.

I felt better when Kissie came bounding around the corner, wagging her tail. She stopped by my feet, looking up at me with big brown eyes. While scratching her head, I noticed the well-used Victrola in the corner. Walking to it, with Kissie beside me, I reached to a shelf for a favourite record. I placed it on the turntable, gently putting the needle in the groove as Aunt Lucy had taught me, and waited for it to warm up. The lively accordion music of Wilf Doyle began to fill the room. Biddy O'Toole's familiar voice sang "Mother Malone." I picked up Kissie and we whirled and waltzed, back and forth, on the soft rose-coloured carpet as if we were in Buckingham Palace and I was a princess.

Although we didn't have a gramophone at home, we did have a big

Silvertone radio that my brothers had bought from Buchans. My sisters and I would hear the music from the kitchen as we danced to songs such as "Among my Souvenirs" and "Button Up Your Overcoat" on the back porch veranda during summer evenings. I missed dancing with them.

Still, Kissie was a good dance partner, but she was growing heavy. I loved Kissie but I drew the line at sleeping with her.

"She will keep you company," insisted Aunt Lucy.

"But she bit me," I cried my first morning there.

"You must be mistaken," said Aunt Lucy, pursing her lips, effectively stopping me from saying anything else about Kissie.

When the puppy grew too heavy, I laid her on a fluffy pillow, where she snuggled down until I could just see her eyes watching me. "You stay, Kissie! I am going to help Aunt Lucy set the table."

I first moved the stereoscope with the wonderful 3-D pictures from the dining room table to the fireplace mantle. The blue porcelain teapot with gold trim was already sitting on the square white tablecloth whose corners were hand-worked with little green cups and saucers.

The tops of the matching, folded napkins peeked from the crystal water glasses like spies. I arranged the silverware as Aunt Lucy had showed me, being careful to put the knife and the spoon to the left of the china plates.

Flaky tea buns, butter made from goat's milk, and Labrador bakeapple jam already prepared by Aunt Lucy and me were waiting in the kitchen to be bought to the dining room table. Although that morning I had only stirred the jam, I already knew how to make pies and churn butter. Mother had taught Lucy and me these things a long time ago.

Before the guests arrived, the cheese, wrapped in white muslin, was rescued from the well by Uncle Ned. It had been placed in the water bucket to keep cool, reminding me of the jelly and custard Mother made for dessert on Sundays at home.

Uncle Ned, after he washed up, popped the shiny stopper from his leather flask to fill it with rum. "Beats church wine," he said as he winked at me.

Although I was sometimes asked to tell a story or a joke when we had company at home, I couldn't think of much to say at dinner at Aunt

Lucy's house. Mr. and Mrs. Pike asked about my family and kindly invited me to visit their home. I often saw Monsignor Dinn at Mass, but never thought of a priest as eating meals. He said Aunt Lucy and Uncle Ned would be lucky to have a girl like me. Aunt Lucy nodded her head and Uncle Ned smiled at me.

"Your aunt is famous for her Labrador bakeapple jam," Mrs. Pike said to me as she reached for another tea bun. "Yes, Lucy sets a lovely table," said Monsignor Dinn, and it is a pleasure to be here to share their good fortune." "Thank you," said Aunt Lucy, "Neddie and I are always happy to see our friends and now Mary also will be with us."

When the conversation turned to the latest news on *The Doyle Bulletin*, Aunt Lucy said, "You may be excused, Mary. Perhaps you would like to play some records in the parlour or look at pictures through the stereoscope while we finish our tea. I'm sure Kissie would love to go with you." That was music to my ears.

Taking the stereoscope with me, I settled down on the couch in the parlour with Kissie beside me. Inserting the pictures into the metal bars of the wooden shaft I peered through the viewer. Looking at pictures of children made me wonder what my sisters and parents were doing today. Were Father and the boys home from the woods early today? Would Pad take Lucy and Ella for a ride in the carriage—perhaps to see me? Father had made the carriage with the boys, showing them how to cut the wood and assemble the pieces. They polished that carriage every Saturday to have it ready for church next day. People came from all around to get Father to make coffins and furniture. He also had a knack for curing sick animals, which earned him the nickname, Dr. Will.

As a cooper, Father made hoops for fish barrels. These were traded in Bareneed for salt beef, boxes of oranges, dried fruit, sacks of beans, peas and flour as well as kerosene oil.

Mother made preserves from berries, vegetables, rabbit, and moose. Blood pudding and fresh butter were staples.

While Father was prudent with our supplies, Mother often filled her apron with jams, fresh cream, and homemade bread, scooting off to fill the coffers of needy families. She was known to put a rock in the bottom of the beef barrel to float the junks of salt meat so Father wouldn't miss what she had given away.

Although Aunt Lucy made cookies and salads for me, I missed Mother's cooking. I hadn't tasted it since last Wednesday, the day Aunt Lucy and Uncle Ned told Mother and Father they would like me to come live with them. Mother had cooked a Jiggs' dinner of pork, cabbage, vegetables, and pease pudding. She also made my favourite dessert, blueberry duff with custard sauce.

After dinner that day, when the stove had cooled, we girls polished the stove again because the very full pot had boiled over. Lucy washed the floor, making Ella and me sit on the bench until it had dried to her liking. She then insisted we wash our faces until they shone. All of this because Aunt Lucy and Uncle Ned were coming to visit.

I jumped when Aunt Lucy gently shook me. I rubbed my eyes and looked around—everything looked strange for a minute. I thought Pad had lost control of the horses. It was only a dream, although to tease us, he would sometimes threaten to spook the horses.

"Mary, dear," said Aunt Lucy, "we are just finishing our tea. When our company leaves you and I will have a look in the treasure trunk in my room."

"I can't wait to do that, Aunt Lucy. I'll say goodbye to everyone. Then, I'll just go upstairs and finish putting away my clothes while I'm waiting for you."

*

My small bed was tucked under the sharply slanted roof in the saltbox house. I wondered how Lucy, Ella, and I would fit in the bed when they came to visit. At home I slept in the big bed with both of them. Sometimes we slept end to end holding one another's leg that we wrapped in a towel, and pretended the legs were dolls. When Father heard this he made our dolls, whittling them out of wood.

The first real doll we had in our house was sent to Gertie when she was the baby by our sister Josephine, when she first went to Philadelphia. We all thought so much about it. But Pad cut the back out of it one day. It was full of sawdust. We were so disappointed. We had thought it might have real parts inside. However, all was well when Father fixed the doll.

I opened my suitcase. The smell from the lavender sachet Mother had put in there reminded me of her bedroom. Trying not to think about this, I carefully hung my clothes on a peg on the wall. Like ours and most people's houses at that time, Aunt Lucy's house had few closets.

That finished, I could only wait for the company to leave so Aunt Lucy and I could look in the treasure box. I sat on the bed. White lace curtains billowed from the open window in the hall, beckoning me. As I wandered towards the window, I saw the closed door of Aunt Lucy's bedroom. I couldn't resist opening the door to take a peek. Blessed Virgin! A bedroom for a queen.

Aunt Lucy had a large feather bed covered with a chenille bedspread with red and yellow roses on it. The inviting peaks and valleys of the mattress was more than I could resist.

I climbed up and began to jump. Slipping sideways, I bumped the washstand which had a jug and basin painted with the same flower design as the chamber pot by the bed. The washstand tipped towards the bed. Hearing the pottery clash together as it tumbled towards me, I froze.

My heart was in my throat. I couldn't breathe. If it was broken, Aunt Lucy would surely send me home. I couldn't bear to think of going home for this reason. I lifted the jug. Thank God it was in one piece. I quickly blessed myself.

Holding my breath I listened for footsteps. Voices could still be heard from downstairs. As I slowly let out my breath, a picture of the Sacred Heart caught my eye. It was the same one that hung in Mother and Father's bedroom at home, making me feel lonely for them. On the bureau, in an oval silver frame, was a picture of a man with a long flowing beard sitting on a chair. A woman in a long skirt stood behind him with her hand on his shoulder. I had no idea who they were, but by the look in his eye I decided I should get off the bed and put the washstand back in order, the way I had found it.

Anyway, I wanted to more closely inspect the square object covered with a fine-knit baby blanket that sat at the foot of the bed. I wondered if it was the treasure box. Popping down, I stubbed my toe on something hard. Leaning over to rub my toe, I saw what it was—a metal grate covering a hole in the floor that opened into the room below. As Father would say, "Jumpin' dyin'!"

I quickly knelt down, removed the grate and fell flat on my stomach, putting my face in the hole. There was the same kitchen I knew, but I was looking down on it. There was the stove beneath me. Butterflies fluttered in my stomach.

Leftover buns from dinner were turned upside down on a green tablecloth and smelled even more delicious than when they had been baking in the morning. I saw two bluebirds worked into the hooked mat by the stove. From up here, they looked like they were flying. Sand-coloured leaves on the wallpaper sparkled in the sun's rays.

I could hear voices—the company was still here. Through the lace curtains on the dormer windows, I could see Uncle Ned and the priest in the doorway of the shed. They were drinking from the leather flask. But I ignored them all.

Over the kitchen door was a framed picture of Holy Mary with her mother, Saint Anne.

The daybed, covered with a chintz spread, barely hid the polished spittoon that Uncle Ned used when he chewed Apple tobacco. Father had one just like it at home. Behind the stove, I could see the edge of the padded orange covering on top of the woodbox, where Kissie napped.

On the warmer oven, just inches below me sat the everyday teapot, warmed by a floral tea cozy. Right beside it, at the very edge of the warmer oven was a silver-trimmed tin, decorated with a picture of King George V and Queen Mary.

At Christmastime, Aunt Lucy and Uncle Ned had given our family a tin like this one. It was filled with mouth-watering English toffee. At home, my sisters and I scrambled for the candy when Mother offered it to us. The tin on the warmer oven was big, in my eye. I really wanted one of these toffees.

Because Newfoundland homes were built with low ceilings to preserve heat, the tin seemed within my reach. Aunt Lucy hadn't offered me a candy. But I thought I could get one without anyone knowing about it. I stretched out my arm and pressed my shoulder tightly into the hole. I strained and bit my tongue between my teeth. Finally, I could feel the metal. My fingers grazed the tin. It moved. But I still couldn't get it. I pushed again into the hole. At last, I felt the scrolled top. I reached again, stretching as far as I could. I squeezed my fingers and thumb together. It moved. But I still couldn't get it. With one more push into the hole I could again feel the scrolled top. I reached again, stretching as far as I could, pressing fingers and thumb together. The tin tipped. It fell off the warmer oven, hit the stovetop, and crashed on the floor.

I scrambled back from the hole and looked down at what I had done. There were buttons everywhere. Big, small, silver, gold multicoloured buttons, on the stove, on the floor, even covering the bluebirds on the mat. The bottom of the tin had knocked the lifter to the floor. The cover of the tin was on the Welcome mat by the kitchen door.

I jumped up, flew down the stairs, grabbed my coat from the peg, and ran out the front door. I ran right through the large puddles of water in the lane. Oblivious of wet feet, chilly breezes, or glances from anyone on the main road, I fled. I ran through Clarke's Beach so fast you could play checkers on the tail of my coat. I didn't stop until I fell into Mother's arms back home.

As Mother held me tightly, she called for Father, who was outside in the potato garden. My sisters came running, too, but I wouldn't look at them. I buried myself in Mother's lap. Father, arriving in a flash, put his arms around both of us until I finally sobbed my story. He stroked my head over and over until I calmed down enough to look up and see the worry lines begin to fade from Mother's face.

"Will," said Mother, "you must tackle up the horse and go tell Neddie and Lucy that Mary is home."

Father left to go to the barn. Mother got a facecloth and bathed my face in cool water. My sisters gathered the towel and woolly slippers and poured me a large glass of milk. Just then, Aunt Lucy and Uncle Ned burst through the door. Their faces were as white as sheets.

"What happened to you?" Uncle Ned cried. "We looked everywhere for you, even in the well."

"We were so scared," Aunt Lucy said. "We didn't care about the buttons. They can be replaced, but you can't."

"We had no choice, Will, but to come and tell you and Maggie we couldn't find Mary," said Uncle Ned. "Our only hope was that she came home to you and Maggie. What happened, Mary?"

I was in Mother's arms. I kept my head down because everyone was looking at me. I felt so frightened I didn't know what to say. I had worried everyone so much.

With Lucy and Ella sitting quietly at her feet, stroking my legs, Mother told Aunt Lucy and Uncle Ned what I told them. I was certain now Aunt Lucy would really be angry because I ran away. I could hardly breathe. Tears were pouring down my cheeks again. Finally, Aunt Lucy just gave a big sigh. I dared to look up at her then. She caught my eye and smiled, then said kindly, "You ferret ..."

*

Mary never went back to live with Aunt Lucy and Uncle Ned. Her sister Ella eventually did. Mary and Ella were always best friends so Mary spent a great deal of time in their house, enjoying all the pleasures Aunt Lucy and Uncle Ned's home offered, including Aunt Lucy's treasure trunk. Another story ...

Anne Galway
St. John's

❧ Ragtime Annie ✿

In the early 1950s and 60s, winters in Bonavista were stormy with lots of snow and very, very cold. This is when the hole in the kitchen ceiling over the stove was appreciated. It was used to warm the upstairs bedrooms in our two-storey house.

There were six of us, three boys and three girls, in two separate bedrooms, and the hole in the floor was in Mom and Dad's bedroom. This bedroom was off limits to us children, as our parents said it was, until we got caught. In that bedroom you could see everything and hear a lot. We would sneak out of our bedroom and into theirs. We would lie on the floor near the hole and listen to our parents' conversation. They thought we were sleeping when we were busy eavesdropping.

Twice a week our aunts would drop by around 7:00 p.m. and stay until 9:30 or 10:00 p.m. Oh, the gossip we heard. No names were left out, so we knew what was happening with all the families—through the hole. Most of our aunts in those days eventually left and went to the USA, usually Boston or Washington, DC. But when they were coming home for a holiday or sending a Christmas parcel full of gifts for us, we knew about it from the hole in the ceiling, but we had to act surprised.

Every one of us had a favourite aunt. I did. Before she'd leave she'd open her purse and take out twenty or twenty-five cents (a lot of money then) and give it to Mom to give me the next day.

Where did Mom put it?

On top of the warmer on the stove, under the hole in the kitchen ceiling.

I can see the change now.

Off to bed I'd go, happy as a lark, knowing I would have money to spend the next day on candies for me and my friends.

We were and still are a musical family, through our Dad's musical talent. He would have his musical friends in on a Saturday night and they would play the violin and the accordion. We would lie there on the floor looking at and listening to them play and sing. Mom and Dad singing—oh, what harmonizing. It sounded beautiful. We learned the words to the songs through the hole in the kitchen ceiling.

At Christmastime, Dad would put on three kegs of rice wine and put them behind the stove in the heat, so they would brew. We could see them through the hole in the ceiling. Dad would have his friends in and pass the wine around, sing, and play music. We would lie there and look and listen to it all. Then he would say to them, "OK boys, last drink for tonight." Then he would get his violin and play my favourite jig, "Ragtime Annie." I would listen to that melody until I could hum it to myself. Now I can play and harmonize it on my guitar.

Many times Mom and Dad would mention something and we would reply, "We know."

How we knew was beyond them. When they asked us how we knew, we would not give away our secret. "We heard it from outside," was our answer.

The hole educated us. Mom always said we were smart.

Phillip Pardy
BONAVISTA

❧ "Marnin Faultin!" ❦

In this account the operative word is "down," as you shall soon see. The incident took place on the morning of St. Valentine's Day sometime in the late 1930s or early 1940s. Around Trouty and other places in the Trinity Bight and on the Bonavista peninsula, children used to fan out from their homes as early as they could muster "to own" some older person. The older person would generally be a relative, a godparent, or some other soft-hearted person of the community. 'To own' someone a youngster had to quickly say, perhaps yell, "Marnin Faultin" ("Good morning, Valentine"), before the other person could do the same (all before noon, of course).

Once "owned," the person would be expected to give the child a small gift—a penny, a five-cent-piece, or a slice of lassy bread even.

Jim and Louisa (Aunt Lou) Clifford lived in a big house. Like all houses of the time, it had a massive kitchen with a master bedroom above it on the second floor. To make going to bed and getting up in the mornings a little more amenable, there was a hole over the ubiquitous kitchen wood stove.

Uncle Jim was a known "fish killer" since he brought in more fish over the years than any other skipper of a fishing venture. He was both respected and feared throughout Trinity Bight. To be such a figure, he surrounded himself with a slew of "sharemen"—such as Mr. Johnson, who lived with his family just up the hill from Uncle Jim. Mr. Johnson was always willing to do chores Uncle Jim might request—a servant one might say, and perhaps unpaid.

Now the Johnsons had a house full of boys. Under normal circumstances the children would not visit the big house down the hill, but this was Valentine's, a time when children of the harbour were given a freer rein to meet their superiors.

One, or perhaps more, of the Johnson boys decided to "own" Uncle Jim. So he set off down the hill. It is not known if he entered the unlocked house and went upstairs to find the older couple or if the maid might have sent him upstairs because the older people were not up yet.

Anyway, the lad found himself in the master bedroom above the kitchen. And in the excitement of "owning" Uncle Jim and Aunt Lou (two for the price of one), the young visitor dallied over to the hole and down went one of his legs. For a short while he was suspended, trapped, between earth and sky. With little difficulty and little hurt he extracted himself and the universe continued to unfold itself.

The war was on and some wag or other was set to reveal a new set of words in his vocabulary: "Did you hear how one of the Johnson boys *parachuted down* over at Uncle Jim's dis marnin?"

The boys are all dead now, but the house with its long kitchen and, perhaps the hole above the stove, still stands—all witness to another time when Marnin Faltin was all important.

Clarence and Sarah Dewling
TROUTY

๛ The Drool ๖

I lived in Tompkins, Codroy Valley. Our house had a vent directly over the kitchen stove. The vent was made of wood, the same thickness as the beams in the ceiling. We never heard many adult stories through the vent, as I think my mother (Dorothy Aucoin) was smart enough to keep her secrets away from our little ears.

However, one night our parents and other relatives were playing cards in the kitchen, when my father noticed water dripping on the hot stove. It would bounce and sizzle with the heat. When he looked up through the hole, he saw my younger brother, Frank, asleep with his face over the vent, and he was drooling down on the stove. I remember them laughing.

We did spend time sprawled around the hole in the kitchen. It was a nice warm place to be while listening to the chatter downstairs. Then it would always come to an end, when one of our parents would come up and shoo us off to our beds.

Dianne (Aucoin) Walsh
Conception Bay South

❧ Them Days ❦

I grew up with the hole in the kitchen ceiling. I remember it at our home in Port Union, Trinity Bay. It was in the kitchen, which made the bedroom above the most comfortable in the entire house. I think the youngest members of the family usually claimed it. When we were young, my brother and I used it until we were a certain age.

My memories of the hole are of being lonely and sad. We were a small family, and my father was away, as a lot of fathers were in the 1940s and 50s.

Mom was a night person, so she stayed in the quiet kitchen. Many, many nights I would lie on my stomach, listening at the hole for some sound to know she was still there. At any movement from the kitchen below, I would swing back into bed.

Other times I would take the same position near the hole to listen to conversations of company. Grown-ups were very selective about what they said in front of children, so we knew so little. It was interesting to hear something through the hole that you could tell your friends the next day.

When I married in the late 1940s, I lived with my husband's parents in Catalina for several years. Theirs was a large home but had only one stove. His parents, who were seniors, occupied the room above the kitchen. Several times between January and March, a glass of water would be spilled upstairs and, of course, the water made its way down through the hole onto the kitchen stove. By next morning that water had turned to slush. I often think back while enjoying all the comforts of my house today.

It is a mystery, but at no time did I take my children to a doctor because of severe colds. None of the family had the flu. I think that word has been invented since that time. Maybe our heating system, or lack of one, worked best.

Emma Martin
Catalina

᠀ Wet Hair Tells the Tale ᠀

I AM SITTING AT my table in Grand Bruit, packing up my home, as we are resettling. I grew up in Burgeo and we had a hole on the ceiling. The hole was in Mom and Dad's room, along with the old brick chimney. Both of these made my parents' room very warm. My sister and I shared a bedroom, as did my two brothers. We took turns looking down through the hole. Dad had a grate put over the hole, so if we stayed really quiet, they would never know we were there.

I remember my baby sister wanted a walking doll for Christmas, that walked when you held its hand. Mom kept telling my sister we couldn't afford it because it was too expensive. Dad worked in the fishing plant. Anyway, I got very nosy that Christmas Eve and looked down through the hole in the ceiling.

Lo and behold, our uncle, who owned a shop, came into our house with a box. When Mom opened the box, there was my sister's walking doll. I crept out of my bed, woke my sister, and told her. After that we couldn't sleep. Mom heard us giggling and came up to find out why we weren't asleep. We told her we were excited because it was Christmas Eve. She bluntly told us, "If you don't go to sleep, Santa will bring you two nothing!"

That Christmas, Mom kept the apples for our stockings in her trunk. We used to put one brother or sister on watch at the hole, while another stole an apple. We would pass the apple among the four of us until it was gone. Needless to say, there were many apples missing, come Christmas.

In March of that same year, my grandfather had a stroke and had to live with us. He could not get out of bed. Mom and Grandmother had to feed him.

Our question to Mom was, "How do Granfer pee?"

Mom would say, "Never mind! You don't need to know that."

Well, that made us more curious, so we went on shifts of looking down through the hole in the ceiling, where we got our answer. I heard Granny call out to Mom, "Get the bottle!" so she got some jar that once had jam in it, I suppose. She took it to Granny and Grandfer did his pee.

How nosy were we?

When Mom's friends came in for a smoke and tea, Mom drove us upstairs so we couldn't hear the latest gossip. That's where we heard who was "sick" (pregnant). That continued until one day Mom heard us and threw a glass of water up through the hole. She discovered it was me peeping through the hole when she saw my wet hair.

Marilyn Billard
La Scie

❧ We Two ☙

I was born in Bond's Path, Placentia in 1954. Our house had a grate in the ceiling over the stove that covered a hole up to my parents' bedroom. That room was the warmest one upstairs because of that.

I remember once a cat got in the bedroom (unheard of in those days!) and, while it was being chased out, it "escaped" into the hole (there was about a six-inch space between the floor of the bedroom and the ceiling of the kitchen). That warranted a bit of excitement.

When I was older and came home for weekends, my father often slept on the daybed in the kitchen in winter and I used his bedroom. He liked to get me up by 10:00 a.m. by turning on jigs and reels on VOCM loud and clear. The smell of bologna and eggs frying on the stove would waft upwards as an additional enticement to get up out of bed.

My older sister, Doris, tells a story about how she studied so hard in school, scared to death of the repercussions from the nuns of not knowing something if called upon, that she would stay up for hours. One time, as she sat there half asleep over her books, Mom put her head right down in the hole in the bedroom and shouted at her: "If you don't go to bed right now, I'm coming down there and I'll burn those books." Our mother was a very well-read woman who valued education, so this is a very funny and fond memory, since she passed away when we were quite young.

We couldn't see a whole lot from the bedroom to the kitchen, since our grate was right over the stove. You could see a little if you tried, but you could certainly hear well enough.

Mary (Collins) Walsh
St. John's

As my sister—Mary (Collins) Walsh—was eight years younger than me and was quite young when our mother died, she may not remember that we opened our Christmas stockings and presents on the bed in Mom and Dad's room as it was the warmest room in the house because of the hole in the ceiling. Our stockings consisted of an orange, an apple, a bottle of Coke, sometimes some grapes and a little bag of candy, usually pink chicken bones, as they are still called. If we were sick and had to stay in bed, Mom would bring us warm milk in a bowl with homemade bread soaked in it and canned fruit—this was a big treat. If the doctor had to come to the house to visit if we were sick, that's the room to which he came.

Doris Collins-Scott
ST. JOHN'S

❧ Seen and Not Heard ❧

It's so strange how one small thing can have such totally different impacts. I grew up in Ship Cove, Burin, in the late 1930s and 40s, and the hole in the ceiling is associated with many memories for me.

My family relied on it to help heat our home. This was back when the only heat came from the stove in the kitchen. Without the hole in the ceiling, every room on the second floor of our family home would forever be too cold to enter. Our trips to the washroom would have been cut down to only going when you couldn't wait any longer. Our early departure to bed would have been like lying on a slab of ice. The hole in the ceiling meant that life during hard times was just a little more bearable.

The hole in the ceiling was where I got an education. Not like the one you get in school, but one that you get from living. As I was the youngest of four, I was banished to bed so early that I never got to participate in anything like my older three brothers did. First, there was Jim, the oldest; he worked in Argentia, and the only way I heard what was happening with him was when I overheard my parents talking— through the hole in the ceiling. Then, there was Kevin who along with my parents and some relatives, constantly played 120s. Many a night, after having been sent to bed, I would lie on my stomach in the hall and listen to them play cards. With the arguing and disagreeing that went on, anyone passing by would swear that the house was in an uproar.

My brother, Gerry, who was a few years older than me, finally got to join in all the fun downstairs when he was invited to play cards with the rest. However, not before I let him in on the biggest news ever. I told him how I had overheard my parents talking about what they were getting me for Christmas.

He was shocked. He never did tell Mom what was going on, because I would have been in big trouble. To the adults, it would have been eavesdropping, whereas it seemed to be one of my biggest sources of excitement. When the mummers came, I got to see them through the hole in the ceiling, dancing, singing, and playing instruments, again having been sent to bed early. When neighbours came to visit at night, I would again lie on the floor in my pajamas until I would heard someone coming up to check on me.

When I had daughters of my own, they spent many of their early summers at my parent's house in Ship Cove. Over the years they have told me how they spent summer nights stretched out on the floor in the hall listening to the sound of the rocking chair creaking back and forth. And how, thinking them to be asleep, the adults downstairs would talk about things that were not for children's ears. They too remember how secretive it felt during those times when they were to be seen and not heard and how listening to the fun and laugher in the house through the hole was such a special treat.

The holes in the ceilings are gone and so are the times when you made your own fun just listening to a game of growl.

Anita Pender (nee Cheeseman)
Kilbride

Submitted by Deborah Horsman (nee Pender)

"Santa Here Yet?"

When I was seven years old, my father died suddenly of a heart attack. At the time, my mother was six months pregnant with her fifteenth child! When my baby brother was born, Mom rearranged her room to accommodate two beds: hers ran along the wall with no window, the other was placed along the window wall. This is where she moved me and my younger sister from "the girls' room." She shared her bed with the baby.

Just over the edge of our bed was a hole surrounded by tin or some other material. It once was where the stovepipe came up and entered the chimney. But by then the pipe had been removed from upstairs and rerouted to the chimney from the kitchen. This became THE HOLE! It provided heat for our room.

When we were supposed to be asleep in our bed, we often watched the goings-on in the kitchen of our home on Empire Avenue in St. John's and listened to conversations from our perch above the hole. Sometimes we put our heads down—we'd get caught. Mom would say, "I thought you two were supposed to be in bed. Get back to bed and go to sleep!"

That year, when I started school just after my father's funeral, I saw a piano for the first time. I fell in love with it and would come home and play on our kitchen table! I knew I couldn't get a real piano for Christmas, so I asked Santa for a toy one. That would have satisfied me!

When Christmas Eve came, I went to bed like I was supposed to.

But I woke suddenly to the sound of a tinkling musical instrument. All excited, I stuck my head down through the hole and asked, "Mom, is Santa here yet?"

To which she replied, "No! Now go back to bed. He won't come until you are asleep."

The next morning when I got my stocking and presents, there was no piano. I was crushed.

Instead, I had a xylophone, which sounded exactly like the sound I had heard the night before, when Santa had not yet come. That's how I found out that there was no Santa, and Christmas has never been the same since!

Incidentally, I did learn to play and love the xylophone, and I still do—to this day!

Dorothy Fitzgerald
South River, Conception Bay

❧ Need to Go ☙

My father's story of accidentally peeing through the hole in the kitchen ceiling when he was a child is surely worth telling.

The need to relieve one's self often is strong enough to wake a person up, but only partially. Such was the case with young Bob, who arose from his bed late one night in Marystown with the intent of reaching the pee pot in the closet of his bedroom. While still in a daze, he confused the hole of the pee pot with the hole in the ceiling. This hole was designed to allow the heat from the wood stove in the kitchen to rise *up* to reach the bedrooms upstairs. It had instead the warmth of pee going in the opposite direction. Young Bob had not reached the pee pot but instead was "going" through the hole in the ceiling. With impeccable aim (for a half asleep child), his pee landed straight into the frying pan!

Maryanne Drake
MARYSTOWN

"Can a Woman Who Was Once Loved Completely ..."

We had a hole in the ceiling in our home in St. Phillip's. It was over the kitchen stove, positioned so the heat would rise to the bedrooms. We were always sent to bed early when we were children. I can understand now but could not then, of course, that my parents wanted some time to themselves. As I was the oldest, I was the last to go to bed. Around that time, about 7:00 p.m., there were several radio programs that I had taken an interest in listening to.

One was *Courtship and Marriage* and the other *Second Spring*. I cannot find anyone who remembers listening to them. Maybe the content was not for children of my age. I cannot remember much about the stories or characters except for the names, and a little of the drama in the stories. I do remember that in one of the stories, people on a ship at sea encountered large octopi. It must have been traumatic to me as a child, because I do remember that scene and how I used my imagination to bring it to life.

I lay rolled in a blanket listening to the radio that was sitting on a shelf, sharing space with an eight-day clock that chimed every hour, on the wall, over the daybed to the right of the stove in the kitchen below. If my mother heard a noise, she would shout, "Get in the bed up there." I would just move aside from the hole a little. As long as my ear was aimed at the radio to hear the stories, I would be OK. Then I would gladly climb into bed. But if a neighbour came calling, I would be out again to see who it was.

Theresa Cantwell
Torbay

❧ Holding Her Own ❦

This story was related to us with gusto by the late Dr. Clare Neville Smith, formerly Provincial Pediatrician of Newfoundland and Labrador, and an immigrant to Canada from the UK.

In her early days in Canada (in the 1950s), Dr. Smith was working with the Grenfell Association at Harrington Harbour on the Quebec North Shore, sometimes travelling by dog-team or bush plane on skis. On one occasion she was being transported by sled and dog team to the next community, and declined the opportunity to retire behind a bush during a break in the journey.

On reaching her destination, she was shown upstairs to her room, and heard an approving male voice coming up through the hole in the bedroom floor: "That doctor sure can hold her water."

Joyce and Alan Macpherson
St. John's

The Internet

I've lived in Port aux Basques all my life. My parents' old house had a hole in the floor in their bedroom right above the kitchen stove. It was about twelve inches by twelve inches and had a fine-mesh screen in it. There was a piece of wood with the flooring covering attached to it so that the hole could be covered over when needed. I guess the hole was there to allow the heat from the stove to go upstairs.

I remember, at least sixty years ago, finding it intriguing to go upstairs and talk to my mother downstairs while she was cooking over the stove. I guess it was our first Internet!

My mother once told me that my father was sick in bed when I was a small child and he wasn't allowed to come downstairs. I wasn't allowed in the room where he was, for whatever reason. He was in that room for several months and the only way he could see me was to look out over the edge of the bed down through the hole.

Joseph W. Roberts
Port aux Basques

~ Sagging Stockings ~

I REMEMBER LYING ON my tummy in my grandmother's room above the kitchen and looking down through the hole, listening to the conversations long after I should have been in bed. This was in Holyrood.

One Christmas Eve, I discovered through the hole that there was no Santa Claus.

My long brown stockings (two, as I recall) were hung on the corners of a high-back chair in the kitchen. I saw Mom filling the stockings. It was a joy seeing those stockings sagging to the floor filled with mostly apples and oranges.

Shortly after this, Mom and I moved to Boston, where there was no hole in the ceiling.

Recently my granddaughter asked me if there was a Santa Claus. Immediately the memory of watching from the hole in the ceiling rushed to mind.

Alice Lee Finn
St. John's

ॐ The Old Anglican Rectory ॐ

This story took place in Bay Roberts many years ago in what was known as the Rectory, a beautiful big home that stood across from the old Anglican cemetery.

The Rectory was levelled to the ground by fire around 1964. If this tragedy had not occurred, the building would have been a landmark today. However, when this wonderful place went for sale in 1951 it was bought and lived in by my family's good friends and neighbours, Aunt Mary and Uncle Herb.

Uncle Herb was a veteran of World War I and Aunt Mary a Scottish war bride.

They were not related to our family but in the East End of Bay Roberts where I lived and grew up children often referred to older people as aunt and uncle as a matter of respect.

Aunt Mary and Uncle Herb's new home was beautiful and, as once befitted the former residents of that day, had a real bathroom, a rare commodity for many people in Newfoundland in the early 1950s. This is where my story from the hole took place.

My mother, often taking me along, seldom passed by the Rectory (as the house continued to be called) without going in for a visit. In fact, it was a stop we made almost every Sunday night after church.

Uncle Herb and Aunt Mary were always jolly, friendly people and a pleasure to visit. On one such occasion my mother and Aunt Mary were upstairs admiring the bathroom of which everyone was so proud. It was directly over the kitchen and had a hole in the floor to allow heat to rise from the stove below.

The women were upstairs chatting and I was down in the big old kitchen with Uncle Herb. His attention kept straying to the 6 inch by 10 inch hole as he tried his best to be part of the conversation that was going on in the bathroom above.

As he was looking up and talking, he decided to light his pipe, which was never far from him. With both his pipe and matches in his left hand, he decided to "light her up." How his demeanour changed when the full box of matches caught fire and exploded in his hand.

Uncle Herb looked toward the ceiling and yelled, "Now, Mary, look what you made me do! What are you up there for? And with that thing open! I got me hand half burned off, maid!"

I can still see Uncle Herb now with the box of exploding matches in his hand. I didn't understand then how he could blame it all on the women.

Gail Snook
St. John's

∽ Dancing on the Bridge ∾

The screen door slams behind me as I run into the back porch. I step out of my rubber boots and run my hands under the faucet. Dried blood and scales and the stench of guts wash from my stained and calloused hands. My wool socks slide over the warm kitchen tiles just as my mother comes out of the pantry. She swings a dishcloth at me.

"What have you been up to, you big galoot?" she shouts.

"What are you getting on with, Mum?" I ask.

I'd been at the wharf and heard that the priest was making his rounds to some of the homes in the community, but I wasn't about to let on that I'd heard of it.

Mother turns towards the window and is distracted by a figure heading towards the house.

"Get up along and don't open your trap!" she says. "Shush! Up those stairs now! The priest is coming!"

I hurry to the top of the stairs and flatten myself on the floor. I press my eyes and nose against the heat vent that is cut into the floor, and watch as she hangs her apron behind the wood stove. She grabs the goose grease rag from the warmer and makes a quick swipe over the top of the stove before hiding it away.

She turns her face towards the stairway. "And don't dare show your face 'til the good Father has left," she orders. As if I'd ever think of it!

I peer through the vent. The floor tiles below are faded but shine from a recent scrubbing and waxing. The news of Father O'Callahan's visit has spread throughout Outer Cove quickly and I suspect that the women were grateful to be warned of it.

As I lay with my nose on the cold metal floor vent, the smell of fresh bread mingles with the dusty heat that brushes my face. Through my own private View-Master, I see the priest enter the kitchen.

"Oh! Come in, Father," says Mother as she gently places a cup and saucer on the table. I recognize it as the good china with the pink and red roses. "Sit down, Father, and I'll get you a cup of tea. The kettle is boiled."

The priest sits at the head of the table.

"Well," he says, "that is very good of you Sadie."

"I've bread fresh out of the oven, Father," she says.

"Just the tea, please, Sadie."

He lifts the china cup, made in Japan, which looks too fine for the likes of his bulky, gnarled fingers.

"Now, Sadie," he says, "I suppose you know what brings me to your home this day."

Mother shifts uncomfortably.

"As you might have heard," he continues, "my man John caught a crowd of young ones late last night dancing and carousing on the Outer Cove Bridge. And on a Sunday, no less!"

"'Tis a terrible thing, Father," says Mother.

"I understand that your young Jim was amongst them. He was seen in the arms of a young girl from the parish."

"I'm terribly sorry about that, Father," says Mother, bowing her head, humbled by the sins of her pitiful son. I take shallow breaths and lay so still that my legs begin to ache.

"Never mind, Sadie. I have a job that should keep him busy for a few days," he says.

I hold my breath and watch the blue veins on top of his head bob toward Mother.

"He'll report to the deanery this very afternoon. There are leaves to be raked and plenty of weeds to be pulled in my garden. That should keep him out of trouble for awhile." He stands and places his hat on his head.

Mother apologizes again for her son's behaviour. "He'll be there shortly, Father," she says. "You needn't worry, Father."

The priest steps from my view. I hear the porch door close, and I slowly rise from the floor. My feet are like two overstuffed pincushions as I hobble towards the hall window. I peek behind the lace curtain and watch the priest lean into the breeze as he heads down the lane, his black robe drifting behind him. I suspect he'll be heading over to Tommy's house next.

I wonder if Julie's mother has received a visit from our Reverend

Father. The lovely Julie with those curly brown locks. I can still imagine the scent of lilacs as we danced on the bridge—the only place flat enough to dance, given the gravel roads and muddy banks in Outer Cove. It was only after my third drink of ale that I got up the nerve to ask her for a dance, but I think that she liked it quite well. I would have got a kiss from her too if we hadn't been forced to run off home, when the priest's man came along in his old tin Lizzie.

"Get down here, you big galoot!" shouts Mother.

I clamber down the stairs and as soon as I enter the kitchen, Mother reaches up and grabs my ear, giving it a twist that forces me to bend sideways.

"You've disgraced me!" she says.

"Sorry, Mum. I won't let it happen again," I answer through gritted teeth.

She gives one more twist.

"No, sir. Never again," I squeal.

She lets go. My ear rolls back in place.

"Sit down and eat your dinner," she says. "When you're finished, get up to the deanery. You've got extra work to do this day!"

Reaching into the oven, she removes a large plate of fish and brewis and places it in front of me. She cuts two large slices of bread and places them on the table, along with a bottle of molasses and my mug of tea.

As I eat, I watch her scrub the china cup and saucer and wrap them up in wrinkled tissue paper that was once white. I hear her move to the pantry to place them into her special cupboard.

I finish eating and head towards the door.

"You come straight home when you're finished at the deanery. There's more work to be done here this evening," she says.

"Yes, Mother," I reply. My ear is still burning.

As I haul on my boots, I wonder if I'll be heading to the bridge this Sunday. That depends, I suppose. I rub my sore ear. But if she's there, I'll have to go along.

Donna Marie Kelly
MIDDLE COVE

CHAPTER 4

The Townie Learns Her Lesson

I heard from da hole ... sure as you're alive dere's a baby on the way.

🙟 The Townie Learns Her Lesson 🙝

It was a late summer evening, August 20, 1938. The light clouds floated like little lambs across the moonlit sky. Millions of stars winked knowingly at us as we sat on a big rock near the turn path just past the church. Teeny heard Dad and Uncle Bill talkin' about the headless man at the turn path near Uncle Jim's well so we'd never go dere. We had just cleaned off every liddick of molasses raisin cake Mom had made for my sister's seventeenth birthday. Of course my sister was not one of us. She was seven years older, so she considered herself one of the adults now. We didn't want her anyway, since she was an adult and adults couldn't be trusted to keep a secret. She would blab everything to Mom and Mom would tell Aunt Pris and Aunt Pris would tell someone else. Pretty soon it would go around the pond, down the shore, past Big Tree Hill, and all around Ireland's Eye.

Like you would, we got to talking about the same old stuff, about who was courtin' who and whatever tidbits of I-knows-something-you-don't-know stuff. Ollie was the first to ask, "Well, maids, what did ye hear in the hole lately?"

Liz was dyin' to get her bit out. "I knows about Marg. I heard Mom and Aunt Emmy talkin' 'bout it last night. I listened thru the hole. I heard Aunt Emmy say, 'Marg is in the family way,' and, sure, she's only fifteen. She'll have to get married now fer sure. My dear, das cut and dried fer dang sure."

"Wait! Wait! What is this hole you are talking about?" asked Lainey.

We all giggled and then Janie yelled at Lainey and said, "Oh, for Gawd sake, maid, don't you know nothin'? 'Tis the hole in the kitchen ceiling, of course!" Poor Lainey had tears flowin' in buckets by this time, and we got some sorry. Lainey was from St. John's and I suppose up there they didn't have holes in the kitchen ceiling. Lainey said they had telephones to get all the gossip. They only had to ring two long and one short and talk, and four or five other people could listen in.

"Well, I'm some glad we don't have dem tings," said Hazel. "Sure, you can't keep a secret with dem tings, my dear."

"Is that why you have a hole in the kitchen ceiling?" asked Lainey.

"No, maid, das the way we warms up the bedroom upstairs before we goes to bed," replied Hazel. "The youngsters listen thru the hole to find out tings, and what tings we hear! Sometimes it'll make your hair curl! We'll show you what 'tis de morra."

Next day, we took off fer de house and up we goes to the bedroom with the hole in the kitchen ceiling. We heard Mom runnin' in and out of de wet, and right on her heels comes Aunt Clara, Mom's sister.

"Well, Clara maid, you just cot me lookin' like a birch broom in the fits. I was out tryin' to get me hay in pooks before the rain comes too hard. Come on in, maid, and we'll have some tea and lassy toutons. To tell ye the trut' maid, I'm feelin' mops and brooms de day. I spose 'tis the weather. I feels like someone sent fer and can't come."

Mom had to shout at Aunt Clara because she was deaf as a pickaxe. That suited us right fine 'cause now we could hear everyting they said.

I looked down at Aunt Clara and she looked like a soggy doughboy, wet from head to toe. The look on her face would scare a dogfish away, too. Poor Mom knowed all about Aunt Clara's complaints. She always called her Calamity Jane, behind her back of course.

"Well, Eff maid, 'tis Jarge and me had the racket de day. Dat gommel is stubborn as a mule and crookeder than a pork-barrel stove."

"Now, Clare, you got ta have more gumption and give'n as good as he sends," said Mom.

"I knows dat, Eff, but I jes got ta bite me tongue and not spake a word. You knows, maid, 'tis not fer the want of a tongue dat a horse can't spake."

Lainey was gettin' on like a cat on a hot rock. She was wettin' her pants from laughin' so much. Aunt Clara and Mom went in the inside room 'cause Mom wanted to show her a quilt she was makin' out of scraps of old clothes. That was our chance to creep out.

When we got back to the rock at the turn path, Lainey was all gung-ho to hear more stories. I told her about listenin' to Mom and Aunt Pris talkin' about someone in the family way.

"Aunt Pris is some bossy and always tells me to go outdoors somewhere. Well, that won't do me, so I pretends I got a headache and I goes upstairs so as I can listen thru the hole in the kitchen ceiling.

STORIES FROM THE HOLE IN THE CEILING

Sometimes dey whispers and it's never a Hant's Harbour whisper, hear it across the bay. I tells the girls and we all watches the clotheslines on Monday washday. Ah ha! Dere would be the hand-me-down baby clothes and the flannelette diapers. Sure as you're alive a baby was on the way! We'd meet at the turn path and laugh our bellies full at how smart we is.

"We all knows she was big as a puncheon, girl. Sure, das as clear as de nose on your face. Dey're some stun' if dey thinks we don't know. Dey can't tell us no more dat babies comes from stumps or dey comes from the big bank in the medder. Teeny dug all one day and she couldn't find nar'n. And what about the stark? Sure dere hain't none of dem round here. Besides, sometimes dey calls Aunt Lottie from the pratie garden and she goes runnin' with two or three more women chasin' after her. Sure, wherever dere's a baby, dere's Aunt Lottie.

"Lainey, my dear, you should hear Teeny tell about the ghost stories she heard thru the hole in the kitchen ceiling. Dad and Uncle Tom used to talk about a ship that went down across the Sound. Every foggy Sunday, the crowd over dere hears men moanin' and cryin' near the land. Then there is this man from across the tickle who used to pilot in the big ships through the tickle on the way up the Sound. One foggy Sunday evening, he went out to guide in a ship. Just when he went to step on the ladder to the ship the lights went out and the whole ting disappears. It frightened the daylights out of 'n and he never went out no more. Now every foggy Sunday after dark some people goes up on the big hill and watches fer the lights of dat ship. Lots of people seen it.

"Teeny took de ghost stories to heart. One day when she was comin' home from school she felt her stomach fall down to her boots. The headless man was after her fer sure. She took off with her heels touchin' her backside, jumped over the picket gate, and fell on the kitchen floor, white as a sheet. Poor Mom almost fell into the pot of lobscouse she was stirrin' on the stove. Teeny was screamin' 'De headless man is goin' da get me!' over and over.

"Dat night we heard Mom tell Dad, 'Bob, boy, we'll have ta stop yarnin' 'bout ghosts 'round Teeny. Dat young ting got eyes like a hawk and ears sharp enough to hear a pin drop across the bay.'"

Well, Lainey went back to St. John's with all her stories about the hole in the kitchen ceiling. Her friends would think she was silly as two odd socks. They would never understand the hole in the kitchen ceiling because townies have never seen anything like that, poor things.

In the months that followed, the news on the *Gerald S. Doyle Bulletin* told about Germany trying to conquer the world. When Teeny and I listened through the hole in the kitchen ceiling, Dad and his brother George would talk about the news. Uncle George would say to Dad, "Yes, Bob boy, the next war will be fought in the air, and dat war is not far off. Winston Churchill is talkin' hard about goin' after Hitler. I dare say our fellers will have to go if England starts a war against Hitler."

In the summer of 1939, the whole community was startled when a small float plane landed near the shore. Two men came ashore and went up on the highest hill. Some were sayin' they were German spies. Teeny went berserk, locked our two older brothers in the house, and ran away with the key. She was sure they were the English and they were comin' for the boys, just like Uncle George said. She was screamin' her lungs out, "Dey're not gettin' my brothers! Dey're not gettin' my brothers!"

It was a sad day in our house on January 23, 1940. My two older brothers, Jack and Archie, had volunteered to go overseas to serve their country. My younger brother and I had the mumps. Mom said they were catching so we couldn't go near Archie because he never had them and he didn't want mumps when he got overseas. We had to say goodbye through the hole in the kitchen ceiling.

It would be thirty-five years later before all six children were reunited with their mother at my house in St. John's. Special moments were relived through happy memories which, to our amazement, revealed more and more secrets and pranks played on each other through the hole in the kitchen ceiling. Mom's revealing smile told us what we sort of knew all along. Our parents were never fooled. We knew they were on to our shenanigans all along, and as adults we could now acknowledge and accept their way of teaching us the facts of life.

Yes, Mom, many of life's lessons were taught and many of life's lessons were learned through the hole in the kitchen ceiling.

Mabel Kean
St. John's

Hockey Night in Canada

Hockey Night in Canada was somewhat less appealing
than the curse words I accomplished from the hole in the kitchen ceiling

With Howie Meeker commentating, the boys all gathered round
Toronto versus Montreal, I was sure not to make a sound

The puck is dropped at centre ice, my lesson now begins
It's the opening of the season and Toronto has no wins

I listened so intently, switching from ear to ear
It was only when Toronto scored that I conquered how to swear

High sticking call for Montreal, Toronto gets a break
He shoots, he scores, now it's time for my icing on the cake

Four to three for Montreal and my head was filled with grime
I prayed to God that Toronto would score and go into overtime

Sittler does a double shift and the Habs get a breakaway
A slapshot from the blue line could totally make my day

The fans were shouting, "Maple Leafs, go warm up the bus!"
I'm lying on the bedroom floor learning how to cuss

To my demise there was no more noise, Montreal won the game
Robinson had a hat trick and I no sense of shame

How they entertained me I guess they'll never know
Even learned the hockey stats from the kitchen down below

Donna Judge Malarsky
SHERWOOD PARK, ALBERTA

ᔕ All Around the Circle ᔑ

Ah, how well I recall it, 17 Patrick Street, my home as a little girl in the late 1960s. I lived there with my mother, Kay, my father, Eddy, and my two older siblings, Diane and Dennis. The house had a big kitchen downstairs with two bedrooms and a back place where little girls who were bad went for a time out. The next level had our living room, a bathroom, and two more bedrooms. The top level, the attic, was the big bedroom that belonged to my parents, my brother, my sister, and me. We lived with my grandmother, fondly called Rene by all who knew her, including her children (and some of the grandchildren), my grandfather, Dan, three uncles, John, Jimmy, and Maurice, and my two aunts, Frances and Elizabeth—the White family.

It was a busy household, with so many people living under the one roof. Every morning before breakfast I would sit in the kitchen close to the stove and watch Rene braid her hair and fold it across her head. It was a ritual she performed daily. That and filling a plastic green pan with a little water to sprinkle upon her youngest son's head to entice him from his slumber.

I can still hear him scream, "Ah Rene what did you do that for?"

"Get up," she'd tell him, "time for school."

Maurice would drag himself to the sink for a quick wash.

I was seven, and Diane and Dennis were nine and eleven respectively. It was Friday morning and I was all excited. I knew what tonight held: a good old-fashioned party in the living room. Of course, little girls were not allowed to attend such a fine gala, but I had a secret, one that I shared with my siblings. Just above the living room was a hole, a silver-type funnel from the stove, aligned perfectly up the middle of that hole, and that hole was in the floor beneath my brother's bed. It was concealed by the bed for fear of someone accidently falling through it. Many nights we three gathered round the hole underneath my brother's bed as if we were campers round a campfire. Tonight would be no different.

It isn't very often a young girl of seven longs for bedtime, but I did that evening. It seemed as if the day would never end, when suddenly I hear Mom's voice calling to me, "Darlene, it's time for your snack. Gather your brother and sister up. I am leaving soon for work at Marty's and I have to tell you the rules before bedtime."

Dennis, Diane, and I sat around the marbled green chrome set and sipped our tea from our saucers, as Mom warned us sternly, "There is a party at the house tonight. There will be some drinking and I do not want any of you out of bed. Do you hear me?"

"Yes, Mom, we hear you," we answered in our best little Catholic girl and boy voices.

We walked to the bedroom with Mom, where she kissed us and tucked us in. She took her jacket and purse and a package of Matinee cigarettes. Then she turned and descended the stairs.

Then it began—the countdown to the party. How long would it take? I wondered. Minutes passed, perhaps hours, for I was only seven, and impatient.

The next thing I remember is being shaken awake by my sister Diane. "Get up!" she yelled. "You fell asleep. Come to the hole."

My brother was already in his spot. I could see his long legs and feet protruding from the bedside. Diane helped me position myself, and they both took care as they held me tightly and lowered me down the hole for my first glimpse of the Grand Gala. How excited I was as I looked around for familiar faces. Jimmy was stood to the side, very macho, leaning against the wall with a cigarette pursed between his lips. Maurice stood below the hole nursing a bottle of Dominion, which he laid atop the stove. Uncle John was sitting, legs crossed, on the daybed in his cream-coloured, fisherman-knit sweater. Quiet as always and sipping a beer, it wouldn't be long before the crowd had him up singing songs, as only John White could.

The music, oh the music. Aunt Frances sat in a chair she had carried up from the kitchen, and beside her was Uncle Leo. They had an accordion each. Frances had a mouth organ attached to her accordion (which reminded me of a contraption used by old-time dentists for those unfortunate kids who had to wear braces). Her mouth was positioned on the mouth organ, held in place by the "dental contraption," and her fingers danced along the buttons of her accordion. Leo played alongside her and his feet danced beneath him, as if he were a marionette. How I enjoyed hearing songs such as "I's the B'y" and "Mussels in the Corner."

"Darlene," whispered Diane rather loudly, "stop moving your feet to the music, you're going to slip out of our hands."

I could see Dad. He was in the centre of the floor dancing. He was funny and I almost laughed out loud. Every now and again someone new would enter the doorway and he/she would be welcomed into the kitchen. Hands would reach out and embrace the newcomer and a drink would be placed before him. It seemed as if everyone had talent—jokers, tap dancers, spoon players. Why, at one point I saw someone haul out an old washboard (hadn't seen one of them since Rene got the new wringer washer). I wanted to stay there forever, hanging from the hole, watching my family and friends. I just didn't want it to end, but end it did. I got the familiar squeeze to my baby toe that meant time's up. Someone else was going down. I must not be greedy. I closed my eyes as I started my ascent back up the hole.

Dianne positioned herself and down she went. I could feel her belly jiggle as she laughed inside. I knew whatever it was that amused her so, she would tell me later. I held fast to that, in the hopes of hearing what other wonderful things where transpiring beneath the hole.

How long we took turns that night, I can't say. I know in the wee hours, when daylight crept into the attic, our bellies were sore from not only laughing and singing but lying upon the floor for so long.

Just last week I brought my twin daughters Emily and Kayly to a movie called *Alice in Wonderland*. Alice is falling through the hole, and what lies beneath the hole is a wondrous world.

I turn to my daughters and say, "I looked down a hole, too, and what lay beneath was a wondrous sight."

"Tell us Mom," they plead, and I begin, "When I was a little girl ..."

Darlene Antle
St. John's

❧ Tricky Memories ✦

Memory is a strange thing. It can be deceiving even when we believe it is most accurate. Lawyers and judges know that eyewitnesses cannot be relied upon absolutely, yet the law allows that they produce the most reliable evidence. "I saw it with my own eyes." That is a hard statement to dispute. "I remember it as if it happened yesterday." And yet, that memory could be entirely false.

I have a vivid memory of an event I could not possibly have witnessed. I thought that in childhood I had witnessed the sea behave in a strange way. One moment the sea was as it always was, then it withdrew far into the middle of the harbour and showed rocks covered with weed and there were fish flopping without water. After that a big sea roared up the beach and covered the lower road. It unhooked stage pilings from their grip on the shore, smashed buildings and carried boats up into meadows and people's yards. It even floated houses away.

Such an event did happen on Newfoundland's south coast, but it happened before I was born. I did not witness it, although I would have been prepared to swear that as a child I must have seen such a thing. How could a child make up something like that? Where did such a vivid recollection come from? I had these details stuck in my head long before I read Margaret Duley's novel. I have no recollection of reading about the St. Lawrence tsunami before I graduated from Memorial University. I have never been to St. Lawrence, the community which did suffer such hardship.

Not long ago I listened to a scientist discuss how memories are formed. He said it was never possible to repeat an event exactly. Every time a story is related it changes slightly, and the more often it is repeated the more certain of events the storyteller becomes. That would explain why an eyewitness is absolutely convinced of the truth of a statement or identification. It does not explain where I got my vivid recollection.

I have my own theory. The big sea which swept over the communities on the south coast made such an impression on Newfoundlanders that they kept talking about it for years as if it had just happened. It was a traumatic event, which for many people took away their homes, and all their possessions and left them facing life with nothing to rely upon. As a child I must have heard the stories and absorbed the shock and the terror those who suffered must have felt. My imagination must have so stirred that I believed adults were relating events in our own harbour of Renews. The sea must have been wild and the tide unusual even along the Southern Shore.

Dolores Bedingfield
RENEWS

Rough Landing

I REMEMBER THE HOLE in the kitchen ceiling in the house by the pond on Jerseyside where I lived for several years during my early childhood. My parents slept in the bedroom above and it was the warmest bedroom upstairs as heat from the kitchen range always kept it warm and cozy.

I recall peeping down through that ceiling hole on Christmas Eve with my younger sisters, hoping that I would get a glimpse of Old St. Nick filling our stockings with goodies. How disappointed we were when we never saw his arrival. Memories like that live on forever.

There were times when all of us little ones were sent to bed early when visitors arrived on weekends to play cards or sing and dance. But to sleep we did not go. We would quietly sneak over to the bedroom with the hole in the floor and watch and listen attentively to the entertainment below. Most two-storey houses had a hole in the kitchen ceiling back then, and are still around in some of the older homes today. Although a hole in the ceiling was quite common, it could also be called a safety hazard.

My son-in-law told me of an incident that happened in their family homestead during his childhood. Their ceiling hole was covered by a grate for safety purposes but it seems that somebody had removed the grate and the baby of the house had fallen through the hole and landed on her bottom. Fortunately, she was not injured during the mishap and today whenever the family mingles together and talks about the old days, the ceiling hole incident is always one to reminisce about. With the onset of modern heating systems ceiling holes became fewer and fewer until they became a thing of the past.

Patricia Power
JERSEYSIDE

Five Hundreds

I can still hear my mother say "Get to bed NOW or I'm coming up there" while we poked pieces of paper down through the hole. They would fall on the kitchen table where the adults played Five Hundreds or other card games on long winter nights. In the meantime, we knew that we were safe because she would rather play cards than eat. Other times we would poke a finger down through the hole, which resulted in somebody in the kitchen either pulling or putting a clothespin on it.

These memories are shared by our Murrin clan of eleven children who grew up in Goose Cove on the Great Northern Peninsula, where a hole in the ceiling still exists in our family home.

Anne Murrin Walker
Goose Cove

❧ Hanging ❦

Thirty-seven years ago I was visiting my grandparents' house in Rocky Harbour with my parents and sister. I was upstairs exploring. I was three years old at the time. I discovered a small square hole in the floor of the bathroom. It was covered with a grate. I proceeded to lift the grate out. Below it was a ceiling tile.

I decided to stand in the hole for a brief period. I felt myself falling. My arms caught above the hole. Thank goodness I was stuck!

My mother, who was standing at the sink in the kitchen below, was startled by the noise.

Immediately turning, she saw a body hanging from the ceiling. No visible head, but loud screams.

So much for the hole that allowed heat from the kitchen to warm the washroom.

Steven Shears and Dallis Shears (mother of Steven)
Rocky Harbour

❧ Taking Turns ❧

I grew up in a little community in Fortune Bay. We had a hole in our kitchen ceiling so that the heat from the kitchen stove directly below could go up to my parents' room. I remember it well as that was the warmest room in the house. My father was away at sea most of the time so sometimes one of us children would sleep in there in a large cot. We couldn't sleep with Mom as there was nearly always a baby in her bed. My sister and I would take turns, arguing more than once about whose turn it was to sleep in the cot. We hated the nights when we had to go back to our cold room on the back of the house. We had to make do with a brick or large beach rock heated in the oven to keep warm.

Vera Frampton (nee Riggs)
St. John's

Uncle Am and the Priest

We had a grate in the ceiling of our old two-storey house in St. Joseph's to allow the heat from the kitchen stove to rise upstairs to our bedrooms. For my siblings and me, it was a place to observe and listen to the conversation of adults in the kitchen after we had been sent to bed. After a decent amount of time, we would crawl quietly to the hole and jockey for our favourite spots.

The nights Uncle Am visited were probably the most memorable. A character from the community, Uncle Am enjoyed regaling my parents and their friends with local goings-on and, when in the mood, a story or two.

One night, when I was about eight years old, Uncle Am related a story about his fishing camp in St. Shott's, St. Mary's Bay, near Trepassey. He would go to fish there in the spring. Together, he and the other fishermen set up camp on the beach while they fished for several weeks.

One night, he went outside his camp to attend to nature's call. Suddenly this gush of wind hit him like a brick—even though it was a star-studded, calm night.

He could see nothing around him but immediately felt excruciating pain and stinging in his right hand. He rushed inside the camp to examine his hand in the light. It was blood red and already starting to fester. When he told his fellow fishermen what happened, they thought his imagination was running away with him, and laughed it off.

Uncle Am couldn't stay to finish out his four-week stint at the camp, so he went back home the next day. Since there were no doctors in the community on a regular basis, he went to see the local priest, who hailed from Ireland. This priest had a habit of going in the back roads putting spirits to rest. He was a great believer in people with "demons" in their past coming back as ghosts after they died.

As soon as he looked at the hand, the priest said ominously, "That's BAD!"

He used a pocket knife to open the wound and out came a black worm. He said the worm was the work of the devil.

That priest must have done something right, however. Am's hand healed in a week.

It seemed the more port wine Uncle Am drank, the more chilling the story. My siblings and I moved closer to the hole, the better to hear. I could feel even more goosebumps on my arms and legs as Uncle Am continued with another tale.

This one happened on the road between St. Joseph's and Riverhead, St. Mary's Bay. There wasn't any electricity at that time, so the roads were dark and spooky. If someone became ill and needed a doctor (when one was available), he would make the journey by horse and carriage on the bumpy and rocky dirt road. There were tales told of the horse, on many occasions, stopping abruptly, after which the carriage door would open and the seat cushion would sink down. However, there was no one to be seen! After another few miles or so, the horse would again come to a halt, the door would open, and the seat cushion would rise up again.

The local Irish priest (who was stationed at St. Joseph's for forty-nine years) would say that it was a poor soul who needed some prayers.

When we reluctantly proceeded to bed, we were frightened out of our wits. Even the clothes in my closet were standing like headless ghosts as I hastily drew the covers over my head.

Kathy Lee
MOUNT PEARL

❧ Look at Me! ☙

BACK IN 1953-54 IN our house on Aldershot Street in St. John's, we had one of those wonderful ceiling holes. This particular one was located in our bedroom and looked down into the kitchen. There was a grate over the hole on the bedroom side and wire mesh on the kitchen side of this delightful view. This hole was like a magnet to us kids once we were sent to bed for the night.

One summer night we were in our "room with a view" when we heard voices from the kitchen. My eleven-year-old sister and I, nine years old at the time, quickly scrambled over for a better look. I removed the grate from the hole and we watched our parents and their company. My three-year-old brother wandered over and stood on the mesh to get a bird's-eye view of the proceedings. The next thing we heard was him saying, "Look at me!"

His blond head flew down through the hole. He straddled the top of the warmer of the kitchen stove. Luckily it was summer and the stove wasn't lit because of the warm weather. My brother was unhurt but there was an awful lot of yelling and screaming going on.

Needless to say, my father, short legs and all, cleared the stairs in a matter of seconds. We were duly reprimanded, me more so than my sister because he somehow knew it had to be me who removed the grate from the hole. We were warned, in very colourful language, never to remove the grate again and we never did but oh, the temptation was always present.

Peter Breen
ST. JOHN'S

Memories are Made of This

As a young girl living in St. John's in the 1940s, I have vivid memories of visiting my grandparents around the bay, in Riverhead, Harbour Grace.

I looked forward to visits in winter and summer. My grandparents, Ron and Julia Shannahan, were delightful folks. He was a sealer who was away in the spring of the year. She was a wonderful cook whose Christmas cakes were a must-buy at the Christmas bazaar.

My grandparents' house was a large two-storey with a washstand in the pantry. The kitchen had an old-fashioned range with a warmer on top. The eating area overlooked the water. In the centre of the house was a beautiful oak railing staircase with various carvings. At the bottom of the stairway was a carving of a horse's head.

The dining room and parlour were used for special events such as large celebrations. A beautiful piano stood majestically in the parlour window and was the centre of attention during those times.

On one of those visits, my curiosity was piqued as I sat in Nan's parlour. Directly above me in the middle of the ceiling was a square opening. Wanting a little closer look I went upstairs to find the hole. It was in Nan and Pop's bedroom, which was off limits to me.

When I asked Nan about the hole, she explained, "Child, it's to keep the upstairs warm."

I thought it was really odd to have a hole in the ceiling of your house. But she told me that I could go up and look down into the parlour if I wished. I told my brother. Many times after that he and I would lie on the floor, remove the grate and watch grown-ups. Of course we were supposed to be in bed by then.

There was one occasion at the hole that was sad for me. When my grandfather was being waked I recall looking down and viewing his body lying in the casket. It was a moment in time I would never forget as I thought about the times he held me and how much I loved him. The hole was never quite the same for me after that.

Gloria J. McHugh (nee Butler)
St. John's

Off the Rocker

I grew up in Conception Harbour and the old home is still there. The hole was in the eatin' room off the kitchen. As time progressed the wall was taken out between the kitchen and the eatin' room. The old family rocking chair sat right underneath the grated hole. My mother, Ann Bride, was a bit of a character who enjoyed a game of cards, was a beautiful singer and, could entertain as good as the next one.

The boys in our house enjoyed a few beers or drinks of moonshine and a good laugh. As Mom went to bed she would warn the boys that it was time for bed for them too. Often the neighbourhood lads would still be there.

One particular night during Christmas, Mom went to bed early. The boys came home with their buddies prepared to have a party. The comedian in the group was sitting in the old rocking chair under the hole in the ceiling. Although Mom tapped the bedroom floor above us several times with her walking cane, the boys continued to make noise. She crept out of bed, took off the grate and reached down with the hooked end of her cane and grabbed the rocking chair joker around the neck. What a fright he got!

Needless to say, when the boys came home late after that and bought along their buddies, no one dared sit in the rocker again. When we get together now to reminisce about bygone days, the stories usually begin, "Remember when Mom …?"

Gordon Dalton
St. John's

Gentle Rain

I was born and raised in a one-hundred-year-old, two-storey house with a slate roof in Hickman's Harbour, Random Island, Trinity Bay. My mother, Lydia Green, raised ten children there. She often tells the story of my sister Pat, who is now fifty-eight years old. When Pat was a little girl, she slept in a bedroom above the kitchen. There was a hole in the kitchen ceiling for the heat from the wood stove to heat the upstairs bedroom.

Like a lot of houses in the 1950s, we did not have indoor plumbing. If you had to pee in the middle of the night, you were supposed to use the "honey pot" under the bed.

One particular night, my mother was getting a cup of tea for an elderly gentleman friend. He was sitting directly underneath the hole in the ceiling. Pat got out of bed when she was half asleep. She squat down, mistaking the hole for the pee pot.

My mother realized immediately what was happening. Being very embarrassed about the liquid that was pouring on the bald head of the elderly gentleman, she quickly explained that one of the children must have tipped over a glass of water upstairs. He was gracious about it and even finished his tea. It is a great memory for our family, giving us many a laugh.

Daphne King
Portugal Cove

❧ Airborne ❦

I was born in 1942, the fourth of eight children. I grew up in a typical two-storey house in Holyrood, Newfoundland.

There were four bedrooms. One small bedroom had the chimney from the hall stove go through it and the room was generally warm. This was the room that had a square hole cut to allow heat from the kitchen to rise and warm the bedroom. I'm not sure that it worked all that well because it was pretty cold in the mornings and we often had to blow our breath on the window to check the weather outside.

I don't remember exactly how old I was at the time, possibly three or four years old and my sister six when it happened. She and I slept in the room with the hole in the floor. We had been confined to the bedroom for a week as we both had German measles. It was common in those days to keep people with diseases isolated, even from family.

One morning during this time I was sitting on the floor dangling my legs through the hole. I was chatting with my sister who was still in bed. She was (jokingly, I hope) daring me to jump.

Well, I didn't jump and I am not sure how it happened but I did go through that hole. Just below, to the left, was the old Waterloo wood stove—quite hot by now. In the corner, just below the hole was a shelf with a clock on it. I guess the shelf broke my fall. Luckily I ended up behind the woodbox, which was beside the stove.

My mother, who was hard of hearing, was busy getting breakfast. She was surprised when she turned and saw me coming out from behind the stove.

She asked, "Where did you come from?"

I simply replied, "I came down in an airplane."

To this day, I have a clear image of Dad, with board, hammer and nails in hand headed up the stairs to board up that hole.

Patricia Kean
Mount Pearl

❧ He Knows ... ☙

I GREW UP IN Torbay and our neighbours were almost like family, so much so that we called them Uncle Willie and Aunt Mame. Their house was my second home. One Christmas Eve, when I was about five or six, I was spending the night at their house. Everyone went to Midnight Mass except Uncle Willie and me. He was telling me that I had better get off to bed because Santa would be coming soon. I wanted to stay up longer and was happy to spend a little more time in the kitchen.

Uncle Willie must have somehow set this up earlier. I am not sure how he did it but probably with a fishing line. Suddenly a doll came dropping through a hole in the kitchen ceiling. Naturally, I was totally surprised and amazed!

Uncle Willie then cautioned, "Now, it looks like Santa passed over the house and couldn't come in because he saw that you were still up."

Well, I was off to bed in record time!

Elizabeth Ridgley
ST. JOHN'S

This was the first story received—and in record time!

ᚼ Leaving for Boston ᚼ

Because children were often not privy to the straight talk of adults, it was typical for me to get my information at the hole in the ceiling of our seventy-five-year-old home, situated at the foot of the river and the entrance to North River, Conception Bay.

Because of my experience listening through the hole for information deemed inappropriate for children to hear, I took up my position one morning as daylight was breaking and the sun's rays poking through the lace curtains on the window in Mom and Dad's bedroom.

My parents were already in the kitchen, sitting at the table drinking tea.

"Mike," my mother said, "we will be missing you so much. The girls and I would love to be coming with you." Even Brownie, our little family dog, was yelping piteously at their feet, perhaps sensing the unusual tension in our house.

"I know, love, but it won't be long before I get work. I'll be coming back for you and the girls, as soon as I get work in Boston and find a place for us to live."

My stomach hurt as I listened to them. I knew my father was leaving that morning to join his many siblings in Boston in an effort to find work. He hoped to work as a deep-sea diver. He had already trained in St. John's when he worked in the Chain Rock area at the entrance to St. John's Harbour.

Mom had told Ellen and me that she was expecting a baby. Since Aunt Lucy, her sister on Bell Island, was also expecting, they decided that, if Mom went to Bell Island while my father was gone, they could help one another. I was happy about that, but sad that my father was leaving.

"If all works out, we will live in Boston. You will also see your sisters and brothers who are already working in Philadelphia. It will be a great venture for all of us," said my father to my mother.

I wanted to ask him if he would be home for my First Communion, but I couldn't say anything from the hole because they thought I was still asleep.

My mother nodded her head as he went to her, held her close, and kissed the tears away. I, too, wiped tears away before they fell through the grate and landed on the hot stove.

Although I was sad to see my father leave, I understood that he needed to find work to support my mother, me, my sister, and the little one who was due in September. (He would be my brother, John, though I did not know that at the time.)

"Now, Mike, before we get Anne and Ellen up to have breakfast of tea and toutons with you, we need to talk about how much money you will take with you."

"Don't worry, darling, I have sixty dollars," he enthused, holding Mom even more tightly, "which will be plenty to get me there and last until I get my first paycheque."

I slowly eased away from the hole.

"Wow," I thought, "we must be rich!"

And we were, in many ways!

Anne Galway
St. John's

CHAPTER 5

Portal Antics

"5" in the kitty!

ತಾ Portal Antics ತಾ

We had a hole in the ceiling. It's still there, in the same place, over the Warm Morning at our home in Holyrood. Although my father installed cast iron radiators throughout the house, supplied by an oil furnace, he also installed a grate over the wood stove in the upstairs floor at the end of the hallway. Our parents' room was on the right and the boys' room to the left of the grate. We had to pass or walk on it every day to get up or go to bed.

Without this portal into a forbidden world, our young lives would have been far less entertaining and endurable. This portal worked both ways. Not that you could hear much of the goings-on upstairs if you were in the kitchen; it was pretty much one-way. It was like an earphone for whoever was upstairs and wanted to listen to the boisterousness or hushed conversations that often took place in a family's kitchen. I say both ways, as parents used it too, especially when we were teens and my brothers and sisters and I would get home late or on rare occasions have friends in. We were aware of this and often listened for the movement of the grate louvre which needed to be open to get the best reception.

I recall being in the kitchen with my older brother Bill, who was more of a rebel than I was. We had imbibed together all night, though I'd not had quite as much as he had. His voice gained in decibels, so I gave him the look and rolled my eyes toward the grate over the wood stove. Dialogue freely spewed by two teenagers who just returned from a night of raucousness in Chapel's Cove, Harbour Main, or Conception Harbour was fodder for my father, who was inclined to lend an ear to the grate. This was proven on some occasions by a verbal lashing either in person or through the protective, blessed grate, depending on how excited and vulgar our teenage repartee.

While older memories of the grate are fewer, they are often more innocent and silly. I used to stand on the grate on a cold winter's morning to warm my little feet.

But far less innocent was the time I hatched a diabolically clever plot to transport kittens via a makeshift elevator from the bedroom floor to the kitchen floor behind the Warm Morning. I was seven to nine years old at the time, but I can affirm that this mischievous, but successful action was practiced and carried out several times over the years with various brothers and sisters.

It was not enough that we could forcibly place one of five or six kittens and young cats into a sock tied at one side with mother's yarn (larger cats were not so co-operative and inflicted wounds to our young hands to express their disapproval) but we took delicious Machiavellian delight in performing this Mission Impossible-esque manoeuvre while some card game was under way (which at the time we only knew wasn't Crazy Eights.) Besides my mother's voice, we were thrilled to hear Aunt Josie squeal, "Eeeeee, why did you lay the Ace? You knew I had the Jack."

Little did they know a conspiracy was taking place just mere feet away. Had Annie, facing the wood stove, raised her eyes a few feet above the card kitty, she would have gazed upon a calico kitty's head protruding from the top of a grey sock being lowered slowly behind the warmer at the top of the stove. And therein was the danger zone—that few feet of space between the ceiling and the shelter of the stove's warmer. If we could get through that no-man's land, we had accomplished our mission and we would revel in sweet success.

It was incumbent on one experienced sibling to aimlessly or nonchalantly fade into the background of the card party and dive behind the stove to off-load the clandestine cargo. Many of the cats were recycled to the disembarkation point and shoved willingly, or not, back into the sock. Having gone completely undetected we chuckled our way to our beds and smirked at our cleverness until we fell fast asleep. And yes, we did put the grate back in place, except once, but that's another story.

J. *Pius Bennett*
HOLYROOD

ᴥ The American Factor ᴥ

When I was a young lass in the mid-1960s I was a very lucky girl because my grandfather and my two aunts lived in the house next door. This was in St. John's. On the weekends I was never sure which house my sister and I would sleep in. This would depend on whether or not my aunts' American boyfriends would be in town.

The reason for our excitement to sleep over was because of the hole in the kitchen ceiling. The hole gave us a full view of all the kitchen activities from the upstairs bedroom. The hole in the kitchen ceiling was the beginning of what we know today as reality TV.

My sister and I would spend hours peering through the hole at my aunts and their friends getting ready for their big dates. The show would start with them deciding what to wear or what not to wear, applying their makeup, and fixing their hair. Then the music would start and the girls would practice their dance routines.

The hole gave us a first-hand view until the American boys came to pick up their dates. The kitchen would go dark and all we could see was the glow of their cigarettes. We knew what was going to happen next, as one of our aunts would come up the stairs to see if we were asleep. We would jump into bed and play possum.

For the next hour we would lie in bed and talk and laugh at the fun we had peering through the hole. These memories are always a topic of conversation at our family reunions.

Our aunts always knew we were playing possum, because they too were kids at one time and used the hole in the kitchen ceiling for their amusement.

Rhonda Peddle
Mount Pearl

Company

YEARS AGO, EVERYONE IN the head of Bay d'Espoir had only a wood stove to heat their homes. Ours had one, an Enterprise stove, all black with white on the doors. It had an attached overhead heater, where we put our wet mittens to dry, and a water tank on the right side. This would be filled with water to warm up during the day, and to be used for anything, washing one's self, cleaning dishes, etc.

It was a chore for Mom to cook the meals and to keep the house warm, especially on cold, windy days in the winter. The house seemed to be freezing, especially upstairs. We always got a ton of coal in the fall to add to an ample supply of wood. Coal was especially good for banking the stove before bedtime so that the hot coals would simmer all night, keeping the stove warm and ready to be stoked up in the morning.

Many a morning we all would crowd around the open oven door to warm up, while mother toasted a loaf of bread on the stovetop for breakfast. Toast has never tasted so good.

As time went on, however, electricity came in the Bay, and everyone converted to the Kemac Burner—an attachment that was connected to the back of the firebox. A hole was cut out to fit the Kemac and it was bolted on to the stove. This unit had a blower on it that would run off a 120-volt outlet. It was also attached to an oil supply, in our case, a forty-five-gallon drum laid on its side on a wooden stand on the back of the house.

This seemed to greatly improve the heating of the house. Wood was still used, and the Kemac put on 6 to get the fire going really good. Then it would be turned down to 2 or 3 to help the wood fire. At night it would be left on 1. However, Dad decided to help circulate the heat upstairs by cutting a hole in his bedroom floor, which was directly above the stove. This hole was covered by a register, like the furnace registers used today.

In those days, Saturday was a very busy day for Mom. She washed and waxed the canvas floors in the downstairs area. She had to have a cake baked for Sunday. The stove received special attention—it had to be spic and span. Even the black stovetop was shining when she had finished.

In those days, Saturday night was card night. Uncle George and Aunt Mary usually came by, and we would all be sent off to bed. One Christmas, Uncle Fred's son, Henry, came home from Nova Scotia for the first time in years, with his mainland wife, Dorothy, and family for a holiday. Of course, they were invited down on Saturday night to have a game of cards. Mom and Dad were nervous about having them down because Henry's wife was a mainlander and they were apprehensive about meeting her.

The usual chores has been done in the kitchen and on the stove, and we were told to be on good behaviour or we would "get a lacing," as Mom would say. Henry and his wife finally showed up. She talked differently, but was a very nice person. Mom and Dad and the company were chatting away. Then came a rap on the door: two big mummers, brown paper bags on their heads, with eyes and a mouth cut out. After a bit of fun trying to guess who they were and a few step dances, they revealed themselves: Uncle George and Aunt Mary.

We were all sent off to bed. We first had to do our pee. In those days, it was in a pee pot.

"Now get to sleep, all of you," were Mom's last words.

After some time trying to sleep, someone got out of bed, probably Virtue, and sneaked out to Mom's room. Next, Marion. I could hear them giggling, so I went out with them. The next thing, Ella was with us.

We were having a great time. Uncle George was a comical sort of guy, and he was telling funny stories and everyone was laughing while playing cards. For some reason the pee pot was in Mom's room, right next to us squirming kids. It must have been pretty full. Someone, maybe me, struck the pot and it upset, spilling its contents on the bedroom floor. Pee ran everywhere. Of course, we had taken the register out of the hole to hear better, so a flood of pee went down the hole.

It was pandemonium. The pee hit the hot stove top with a sizzle—and smell. Mom became frantic. Dad was "Jumping Judas"-ing, and the company at first shocked, began to laugh and laugh. We all scrambled back to bed, frightened of what punishment we were about to get from Mom. After rushing around with mop and bucket, and cleaning up the stove, Mom and Dad settled down, thanks to their company.

We were threatened: "Go to sleep, or you're going to pay for it in the morning." I expected to pay for it in the morning anyway. It must have been terrible for our parents. The card game could not resume because of the interruption, so the company went home early. What a good first impression for their mainland guest, who, incidentally, became a good friend of Mom's.

Roger Willmott
LUMSDEN

❧ The Scuttle ❦

I was born in 1941 in Clarenville. We had a hole in the kitchen ceiling—a point of attraction for me and my brother. The hole was also known as the scuttle. I have no idea why it was called this, but more than once we were shouted at to "get away from the scuttle."

One evening my grandmother's sister came to spend the night. Our homework was done, our night lunch eaten, and we were ready for bed. We stayed in bed long enough for Mother to go back downstairs. While their conversation was not interesting, it took a turn for the better when Aunt Rene said to my grandmother, "Last night, I thought I was dying."

My grandmother replied, "Oh my."

"But then I never died before to know what it feels like," said Aunt Rene.

It was hard to keep back the laughter, and laugh out loud we did. Mother soon appeared and put us in our place and made sure that we stayed in bed!

Growing up, we boys would often brag about whose house had the longest and largest icicles hanging from the roof. We now, of course, know that the larger and longer the icicle, the greater the heat loss.

Tony Strong
St. John's

❦ The Pail ❧

One night after supper, my mother-in-law was hooking her mat on the frame. Her son and two daughters were doing a puzzle. Pa (my father-in-law) came home after having a few drinks, ate his supper and went to bed.

Shortly after, he wanted to pee. There was no indoor plumbing then. He reached his hand down through the ceiling hole and grabbed the clothesline. Mom had foster children, so overnight the flannel diapers were usually hung to dry for changing during the night.

When he grabbed the clothesline, he thought he had the handle of the pail. Anyway, the line was going up and down, with diapers flying all over the kitchen like white doves. All you could hear was PST PST PST as the pee hit the hot stove. The smell made whoever was in the kitchen run for the door.

That was sixty years ago in Torbay and we still speak about the night Pa came home drunk and peed through the hole. All he said was, "I thought I had the pail!"

Jeanette Holwell
Torbay

ಶಿ The Comfort Stove ಶಿ

I GREW UP IN Joe Batt's Arm during the 1940s and 50s, the son of a fisherman, in a large family of ten. Like most in the community in those days, we had very little in the way of material things, and I guess by today's standards we lived in poverty. We, of course, didn't look at it that way, and poverty can be a state of mind depending on what is needed to live a happy and contented life.

We had a hole in the upstairs floor, right beside where the chimney from the Comfort wood stove in the kitchen/living room came up through. The purpose for it, of course, was to allow heat to rise up to the four bedrooms off the hallway above. I was a very nosy kid, so they tell me, and after I'd been ordered off to bed, I would on many occasions sneak to the hole, peer down, and listen to what was going on. That was very much the case if there were "cruisers" (visitors) in the house. On many occasions, particularly during the winter months, my mother and father would have three other couples over for cards and a Scoff. The men would play cards, and the women would sit around the stove, knit, gossip, and tend to the cooking. This was my favourite time to eavesdrop and listen to the goings-on.

Apparently when I was quite small I fell down through the hole and was caught by one of my siblings before I hit a pot of hot soup that was on the stove. I have no recollection of this, so I'm not sure if it's true or not, but apparently they made the hole smaller after that to avoid it happening again.

I found this part of my childhood upbringing very funny to relate to my grandchildren, but then again they just cannot grasp what life was like growing up in outport Newfoundland during that period.

Owen Brown
St. John's

❦ The IWA Strike ❧

Almost every two-storeyed house in our community of Hare Bay, Bonavista Bay, had them. Most of the fishermen/loggers called them scuttles. Scuttle is another name for water barrels used in logging camps and on the decks of schooners. There was one mug for all to drink from. It was a great place to hear the latest, hence scuttlebutt.

The hole not only carried heat upstairs but also smells and smoke. When my father lit our kitchen stove on cold winter mornings, a trace of birch rind smoke came up through the hole. My mother's homemade bread toasting in the oven wafted to my nose, just before she called through the hole, "Time to get up, my son." It is a cherished memory.

In our case, the hole was cylindrical and only about four inches in diameter. It was just to one side of the kitchen wood stove, and exited the ceiling into one corner of my bedroom floor. The view from above—though I frequently stretched out on the floor and tried my best to see—was limited. At night the light from the oil lamp on the kitchen table shone across my mother's straight leg extending out from her squeaking rocking chair. Her chair was next to the stove and directly below the scuttle. I could see her nimble fingers flash the white needles, their familiar clicking lullaby assuring me that I would have new mitts in the morning. My mother could knit a pair of new socks or mittens in one winter's night!

My father sometimes toasted bread on the top of the wood stove, using a hand-held wire toaster. My mother didn't approve because the crumbs always burned. More smoke for the hole! She preferred—and so did I—the thick bread toasted in the oven. It took longer but was always golden brown when removed by her fingertips, which never seemed to mind the heat.

I remember my logger father and his logger friends talking about something called an IWA strike. I had no idea what it meant. Their talks sometimes got heated. Blue-grey tendrils of smoke from their hand-rolled Target tobacco cigarettes—a scent I loved—rose through the hole. Here I also heard that a young policeman, William Moss, had been killed in Badger. The men talked quietly after that. It was in 1959 and I was ten years old.

Sadly, the old two-storey house by the side of the dusty road burned to the ground. By that time the hole has been long covered over. Our house was two storeys, with double top and bottom bay windows. It had a staircase with thirteen steps, which I counted every morning as I thumped down over them. The stairs ended at the "inside place" (livingroom) French door, and the kitchen door opposite. There were four bedrooms upstairs, always drafty in winter. The kitchen wood stove was the only source of heat in the house.

Before she went to bed, my mother always "douted" the firebox with the last of the teapot dregs. She walked me up the stairs, a small lamp showing our shadowed way, tucked me under a mountain of homemade quilts, kissed me good night several times, and returned below with the light, and left me staring at the warm glow emanating through the scuttle in the ceiling.

Gary Collins
HARE BAY

Winter Logans

I spent the first fifteen years of my life in Pacquet, White Bay. My father built a house, one storey, around 1939. He wasn't married at the time; he went away to work but returned in 1941, the year I was born. It was the coldest house in the district. He would get up in the morning, light the fire, and go outside to get warm. This was in January. In 1950, with three children, he decided to "rise on the house"—build a second storey.

He cut a hole in the ceiling but, because the original house had a 10-foot ceiling, the hole was about two feet square, and in order to look down you practically had to stick half your body down to see what was happening in the kitchen. The hole, as well as the stovepipe, was in my bedroom, so during the day there was lots of heat upstairs.

My father was scared of fire, which explained the knotted rope that was in my bedroom. In case of fire I was to beat out the window and slide down the rope. Every night he would pour water in the stove to make sure there were no sparks left. My father died in 1955 when I was fourteen, my sister eleven, and my brother nine.

My mother was at a church gathering, my brother was sitting at the kitchen table learning his lessons. I came in and went up to my room, still wearing my winter logans, the ones with all the laces. I pulled up the grate, took off my boots, tied my laces together and silently lowered one of my logans down and let it touch my brother on the head. By the time he reacted I had pulled my boot back up. I waited awhile and did it again. He put his hand on his head and looked around but could not figure what was going on.

The third time he jumped from the table and ran up the stairs and into my room yelling like mad. I was unable to get the boot up in time and he caught me in the act. I could handle him because I was much bigger, but when my mother came home it was a different story. My backside is still stinging.

Ed Norman
Port Anson

After School

Last April, I celebrated my eightieth birthday. My mother died when I was nine years old. My father, who was still a young man, had to go to work, so he left me with my elderly grandparents. They and my aunts and uncles raised me.

I can remember the hole in the kitchen ceiling above the kitchen stove. My cousin and I would go to the bedroom and make dolls and doll's clothing, sometimes after school and usually on Saturdays. Then it was all put away because the next day, Sunday, was God's day.

Here's a poem I wrote about that:

Hole in the Kitchen Ceiling
I remember the hole in the ceiling so long ago
Where the heat from the kitchen could rise from below
To warm up the bedroom on cold frosty days
After school, in the evenings, we'd go up there to play
When homework and study was always all done
Our books put away then we'd have fun

We'd get out our dolls, material, and thread,
Make clothes and quilts for dollies and their bed
Then we had lunch, cup of tea and lassie bread
When we got tired, put on nighties for bed
Off to dreamland, wrapped in quilts oh so warm
But first say our prayers so we'd come to no harm

Hope you like it, Love & Prayers
Myrtle Tippett.

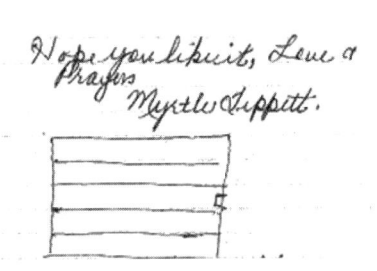

I also remember at Christmastime listening for Santa Claus, but falling asleep before he arrived. I'd make sure the grate was in place because Santa might get in the hole and not get out. The hole was also useful when I was sick with chicken pox, mumps and measles.

Myrtle Tippett
ST. JOHN'S

Editor's note: Sadly, Myrtle Tippett passed away on May 20, 2010, at the age of 80. Though she wrote many poems and stories over the course of her life, this is her first published story.

Burnt Toast Remedy

When my father was a boy growing up in the 1940s, he lived on Merrymeeting Road in St. John's in a duplex home that was shared with another relative and their family. His parents heated their home with a wood stove that was later converted to oil. The upstairs was heated through a hole in the ceiling, which was located directly above this stove. This hole was situated in the boys' upstairs bedroom and provided a nice cozy atmosphere for five young boys. As was customary in most homes back then, a pee pot (sometimes called a commode) was also kept in the bedroom and was used regularly to relieve bladders at night rather than heading down the hall to the bathroom.

One morning when the boys awoke full of energy, they began to skylark about the bedroom.

Someone bumped into the pot and it emptied down through the hole and on top of the stove. The steam, which was emitted throughout the kitchen and the entire home, was more than breathtaking.

My grandfather came up with the idea to place bread on top of the stove to change the aroma into burnt toast. If nothing else, it masked the terrible odour.

There was also another hole in this house—it was situated in the wall which divided this duplex that was being shared with my father's aunt and uncle and cousins. This particular hole held a telephone, which sat on a swivel for easy access to telephone calls being received by both families. It was both convenient and cost-effective.

Donna Winsor
Conception Bay South

❧ Life's Lessons ❧

We are the Wade family (Mary, Joe and seven children) from Conception Harbour, Conception Bay. Our house was a white, two-storey. We spent a lot of time in our kitchen and, when visitors came, everyone gathered around the kitchen table to eat, drink or just chat.

Our main source of heat until recent years was our wood stove in the kitchen. Just above the wood stove in the ceiling was a square hole approximately ten by ten inches. Its main purpose was to let the heat go up to the second floor. The hole was covered by a thin wooden grate with holes in it.

When we were young children and visitors came to the house, we were told to go upstairs because it was a get-together for grown-ups, and no children were allowed. My brothers and sisters would scatter upstairs but I would go to my parents' bedroom where the hole was, lie on the floor, listen, and look down on everyone in the kitchen. There were also times when my parents were discussing problems, or financial matters, and we were not allowed to listen. So, up to the hole I would go to listen to what was happening.

That's how I found out things. My parents rarely told us anything.

I was very careful not to make any noise, so they didn't know I was listening. I was very afraid that if I touched the grate it would move and I'd fall down through the hole. I always had a fear of falling through the hole and being exposed.

It's funny now when I think about it.

After I moved away from home, my sisters and brothers kept the tradition alive, taking my spot on the floor peering down through the hole. With the installation of electric heat, the hole was covered over—no more spying!

My brothers and sisters have all grown up now and have moved away from our family home. Our house is over one hundred years old and is still in good condition. My mother still lives there. The kitchen is still the main gathering spot. No matter how many of us are there visiting with kids in tow, we all stay in the kitchen to chat. The wood and oil stove is still in the kitchen. Nothing tastes better than food cooked on a wood stove.

My grandparents, Anne and William Wade from Conception Harbour, lived just a few houses away from our house. They also had the same set-up in their kitchen. They have long since passed away and the house torn down. The hole in the ceiling remained there until the house was demolished.

Eileen Keating
ST. JOHN'S

The Cozy Hole

The Cozy Hole was a square hole in the ceiling in our kitchen above the oil stove. The heat from the stove would rise into our room in the winter to keep us all cozy and warm. Sometimes, we slept three to a bed.

It was such fun to lie on the floor on our stomachs and listen to adult conversations when there was company in the kitchen in our home on Cabot Street in St. John's. We were all supposed to be asleep in our beds. We had to be so quiet that we could only whisper, in case we were found out. There was always jostling for position for the best spot. Most times, you had to elbow your way in. If you didn't get a good spot, you were constantly asking, "What's going on?" But you didn't get an answer. They'd only wave you away. Everybody else was trying to listen. Not one of us was going to give way to the other.

When we got up feeling very groggy in the morning we had to skirt the Cozy Hole or, before you knew it, your leg would be hanging down over the stove. That woke you up real fast. And sometimes it hurt.

We always knew whether it was Mom or Dad who was the first one up to light the fire and we waited till the heat started to fill our room so the floor wouldn't be so cold on our bare feet. If they were late getting up some mornings to light the stove, we had to hop from the bed to the floor and haul our school uniforms on, fast. It was so cold.

In the summer, when the stove was not lit, we would play a game of pulling each other up and down the Cozy Hole. It was a game to see who could keep their body the straightest while being pulled up and down. We'd play that for hours, or until one of our parents caught us.

It was a great place to spy on your sister's or brother's current boyfriend or girlfriend too. And use that information later to get something you wanted from them.

Oh the memories of the Cozy Hole. It brings me right back to my safe and warm childhood.

Isabel Croke
St. John's

⁂ Mischief ⁂

I too grew up in a house with a hole in the ceiling between the first and second floors. This was in Wesleyville, Bonavista Bay, in the 1940s and 50s when I spent some time by the hole in the kitchen ceiling.

The old kitchen range was the only source of heat. It provided some heat to the upstairs through the hole in the ceiling, a place for mischief and where you learned some of the facts of life. We children could look down through the hole and get a bird's-eye view of what was going on in the kitchen.

I remember the Christmas tree getting decorated on Christmas Eve night. In those days, it was customary to decorate the tree on Christmas Eve night. Because of the hole we got an early peep at the tree. We also knew when Santa arrived and departed our house, so we would be on our best behaviour.

Sometimes we played games through the hole like cowboys and Indians, hide and seek, and fishing. We would draw outlines of different sizes of fish and hook them through the hole. I swear I caught some of my biggest fish that way. When I got tired of that, I was known to hook the hat off an old gentleman's head when he happened to visit and chose to sit about in line with the hole. Can't blame him for getting irritated, but not as much so as our mother who outlawed the hole after that but just as quickly forgave our antics.

Perhaps the most fun was trying to scare one another to death. Just before bedtime, one of us would look up towards the hole and say, "Look, there's someone up there looking down through the hole." We would work ourselves into such a state that we would be grabbing on to one another. With no electricity, just the old kerosene lamp, we would be afraid to go to bed. Mother would drive us on to bed, telling us, "Get away with your foolishness."

George J. Sturge
PARADISE

❧ Rescue Aborted ❦

THINKING OF THE HOLE in the kitchen ceiling in our house in Hickman's Harbour on Random Island brings back a strong memory from more than sixty years ago.

I was probably between four and five years old and my little brother was around two. As kids we were not allowed downstairs in the morning until the fire was in and the kitchen warm, so we often got out of bed and played in the room while we were waiting.

That day, I remember seeing my brother playing with a curtain rod. He backed up, and suddenly just fell into the hole.

He held on for maybe a few seconds. I didn't know what to do. But instead of trying to pull him up, I raced for the stairs. When I was halfway down, I heard a loud thump.

I can still hear that sound my little brother made when he fell through the hole.

My mother was out in the back porch getting wood. She raced in when she heard the noise. The porridge she'd been cooking on the stove was all over the floor. I cringed in the corner, afraid I was in trouble.

But Mom never asked what happened. She knew he fell, and, thank goodness, no bones got broken. Why he did not get burned, I do not know; maybe because she had just put in the fire and the stove had not heated up. I never did tell her that he held on for a few seconds and I may have been able to rescue him. I've carried that secret until now.

Pearl George
MOUNT PEARL

∾ Bum Start ∾

IN THE 1950S AND 60s I grew up in Calvert, a small outport on the Southern Shore. I have lived in St. John's since then, but I have never forgotten my outport roots. I now own our family home, which was built around 1897-98. It is a mansard roof, two-storey house which has undergone many changes over the years. When I was growing up, the hole in the ceiling was actually in our living room, due to renovations.

There were six children in our family: Ernest, Ray, Marie, Francis, Sheila, and me. We all had fun talking through the hole, throwing things down the hole, and even fishing through it. Our favourite story about the hole actually occurred when Ernest, my oldest brother, was around two or three years old. At that time the room with the hole was still the kitchen and Mom and Dad were there chatting with some friends. Next thing, they heard young Ernest, who was up in my parents' bedroom, calling out to Mom asking her to check and see if his bum was clean. He then proceeded to stick his bum over the hole for her to check! We still get a chuckle from hearing that story, except Ernest, who laughingly denies it ever happened.

Last week we were renovating and when we removed the twenty- or thirty-year-old carpet in my parents' bedroom, we found the hole in the floor! It was eight inches by four inches and had been blocked in many years ago. The hole never did have a grate, to the best of my knowledge. Evidence of the hole in the ceiling has been absent from downstairs for many years, although it was still there after the open beams were covered up in the early 1960s.

After our pantry was converted to a kitchen, a brick chimney went right up through the girls' room. It kept our room pretty warm although we still used heated birch junks and hot water bottles to get our beds warm. We still hated to touch our feet to the floor in the morning because it was so cold without electric/central heat. That chimney also saved me from being pushed out of bed many times by my younger sister, Marie. She would put her feet to my back and push and I would have to stick my feet on the chimney in an L-shape to stay in. She couldn't stand having the light on while I read. In addition, my breathing annoyed her so much that it merited a push as well, on occasion, but mostly she just told me to stop breathing! Oh, the joys and tribulations of living and loving in a large family.

Lorraine Croft
ST. JOHN'S

Elizabeth and Archie Get Married

This story happened in the early 1980s in a little town in Newfoundland. It was the wedding day of Elizabeth and Archie. The groom was from a small town on the south coast. The young couple were married in the groom's hometown, and the "time" was held at the home of the bride's parents.

This house was an old two-storey, shingle-sided with a steep, felt-covered roof. Although it had electricity, sewer services were not available, so a pail was used until the town extended its water services a few years later.

Uncle Phal, the father of the bride, was a middle-aged man who had a hot temper when crossed, and emphasized his words by thumping his fist (usually) on the kitchen table. Aunt Rita, the bride's mother, was pretty much cut from the same cloth, temper-wise and colourful vocabulary.

The house was heated by a heavy, cast iron wood stove with a warming oven over the top. To help heat the upstairs faster, a hole was cut in the ceiling and grated over, directly over the hot stove.

It was early in the evening and everyone showed up for the time at the house. Drinks were soon passed around and stories were told, some true, some stretched a little, but everyone was having a good time in the tiny kitchen, especially Brenda, Uncle Phal's sister who arrived at the house already tipsy. Brenda liked her pints as well as any man.

After many pints had been consumed, Brenda needed to relieve some kidney pressure; she carefully made her way up the narrow steps leading upstairs, down a short hallway, and into a small room where the pail was kept. The room was next to the grated hole in the floor, just a couple of feet away.

Downstairs, the party was in full swing, and many were feeling the effects of one too many when there was a heavy thump on the floor above their heads. All eyes went to the hole in the ceiling, wondering what the hell had happened. We soon got an answer when liquid cascaded down through the ceiling hole and onto the stove which, fortunately, wasn't hot.

Apparently, as Brenda unsteadily tried to settle herself on the steel throne, the pail slipped out from under her, causing her and the pail to spill onto the floor, with the pail's contents running across the floor and down through the grated ceiling hole.

Now when your brain is a bit numb from drinking a tad too much, it's a little slower comprehending just what you're seeing coming down through the ceiling hole and the aroma associated with it, but when it does sink in, it will be screaming, "RUNNN!"

It's amazing how fast a person can sober up when you're crowded into a small kitchen and suddenly the contents of the pee pail starts pouring down through the ceiling, hitting the top of the stove, and splashing across the kitchen. Like flipping on a switch, everyone at the same time raced to the narrow door leading outside, getting jammed, pushing and shoving, some with their drinks still in hand trying to claw their way through their buddies, and one poor woman at the back yelling, "HOLY JESUS, LET ME OUT!"

Standing by the stove was Uncle Phal shaking his fist at the hole in the ceiling, fit to be tied, and swearing like mad at the culprit that could have done such a terrible ting.

By this time, Uncle Phal's wife, Rita, had fled up the stairs and was heard very clearly saying what she thought of this awful mess and the one who had made it, at the same time looking frantically for something to throw on the floor to stop it from spreading even farther.

Everyone was outside now, laughing, joking and retelling what just happened. I noticed that most everybody was still holding on to their drinks, as if nothing outside the ordinary had happened. I guess this is one wedding the young couple won't soon forget.

The old house is gone now, replaced by a modern home, with electricity and running water, but there's one thing missing: a hole in the ceiling, right above the stove.

A. Dominix
BELLORAM

CHAPTER 6

The "Hole" Truth

Hold tight till we say good night

❧ The "Hole" Truth ❧

Cradled protectively by two prominences of rocky hills, as if in the arms of Morpheus, lies the tiny community of New Perlican, the quiet, serene place of my youth. On the south side of the harbour, perched on a cliff overlooking Trinity Bay, is my family home, long desolate, sitting forlornly like a widow in waiting. I visited this abandoned saltbox recently and gazed through the cracked windowpanes at its innards. The once-majestic homestead sat like an old dusty photo album whose yellowing pages have not been turned for a long time.

Typical of the homes for that period was a hole in the ceiling. This allowed heat to travel from the wood stove below to the sleeping chambers above. My home was blessed with not one but two such holes in the ceiling. One, in the floor of the back room, peered into the living room below. My siblings and I spent many hours peering sheepishly through this hole, grate removed, spying on the unsuspecting people below. But the real excitement occurred in the kitchen, so the best hole was the hole in the floor of my parents' bedroom.

Peering through cupped hands into the tiny kitchen, I was swept away by a tidal wave of memories. It was forty Christmas Eves ago when my two older sisters, Debbie and Bonnie, and I had sprawled across the floor of our parents' bedroom spying on that same kitchen. We knew it would be a long night of laughter, music, and dancing. Betty and George, our cousins, had arrived and the party was about to begin with Betty's melodic voice and George's guitar picking. A lively rendition of "The Tiny Red Light" soared up through the warm air as we peered into the aperture in the floor. The three of us lay suspended, like cherubs floating on a cloud. What naughtiness would we witness in the abyss below?

The homebrew barrel, sitting stately on its throne behind the stove, was uncovered by my mother's hands, to reveal its frothy delight. Bonnie's face flushed, recalling last year's escapade when she secretly delved into the forbidden barrel. We knew it would be many years to come before she repeated that experiment, preferring instead to leave the merry drinking to the adults below. Little did we realize though, that tonight's adventure would find our mother uncharacteristically exploring the barrel's brew.

The merriment continued throughout the night and the ruckus got louder and louder. Patsy Cline's "I Fall to Pieces" gave way to Johnny Cash's "I Walk the Line," while my mother dipped more frequently into the barrel.

Hours later, when Betty broke out with "How Far is Heaven," we knew the crowd would soon stumble into the cold winter air outside. Our night of spying would soon end. It was then that we heard our mother's homebrew-inspired voice singing goodnight to all as they left. It went something like:

Goodnight to George and Betty,
And Roy and Enid too,
And Harriett and Max, and Joe,
And Blanche and Blanche and Blanche,
Harriett peed in her pants,
So did Betty Bryant,
Enid done it too.
So look out boys for the wash tomorrow!

I can recall looking through the ceiling hole at our mother who was now doubled over in a fit of laughter, legs crossed trying frantically not to pee all over our kitchen floor.

My sisters and I scurried off to bed anticipating the morning, when Santa would make his way to our house, our mother's voice still singing spiritedly in our ears. The best gift that Christmas, we knew, would not be found underneath the tinsel-laden evergreen. It would be in the special surprise of seeing our mother letting it all go (so to speak) and providing us with a family anthem that would be sung at many gatherings thereafter. My sisters and I sang it softly to each other as we giggled ourselves to sleep that Christmas Eve so very long ago.

Webster may have defined a hole as an area where something is missing, but this definition is not as complete as Mr. Webster may have thought. Without a doubt, an addition is needed. Might I suggest instead:

"**hole** *n.* 1. a space (such as in a ceiling) filled with an abundance of magic, mischief, and delight."

Such was my hole in my ceiling.

Connie Peddle
St. John's

Up the Depot

I know it was winter because I remember being pulled on a coaster across the harbour to the bottom of Stanhope. I don't know why it was called "up the bottom" because it is the top of Stanhope. That always confused me! Although we lived in Stanhope, three miles from Lewisporte, I was born in Lewisporte. I popped out weighing ten and a half pounds. My sister Lavinia was four and a half years old when I was born. My mother once told me that for about three minutes she thought she had a son.

The doctor said to her, "Bessie, maid, you have a boy," and then said, "Oh no, it's a girl."

Maybe it's wishful thinking but I never noticed any disappointment in her voice as she told me that story many times.

We were on our way to the depot in Bishop's Falls. Everyone referred to it as "up the depot." Uncle Charlie Fudge, my father's brother, was a woods contractor for the A.N.D. Company. My father was a cook in the Staff House up the depot. Uncle Charlie gave my father the opportunity to live with his family for a year up the depot in the Staff House.

I was dressed in a one-piece brown snowsuit, with a blanket wrapped around me. I remember my face was cold. I was about five years old. I was pulled on the coaster up the bottom because snow had blocked the road down to Stanhope.

A car picked us up there and took us to Notre Dame Junction to get a train to take us up the depot. I don't remember too much about the train ride. My mother told me I fell asleep ... all that fresh air! However, I remember crossing the train trestle and seeing all the water running underneath. Our home in Stanhope was a three-bedroom bungalow. When I first saw the Staff House where we were going to live, I looked in awe because the two-storey house was so big.

The Staff House was where the cooks and cookees lived. This was where meals were prepared for men working in the woods. I can still see my father standing in the doorway, wearing a white shirt and a big bib apron, blowing a cow horn to alert the men that the meal was ready. I would try to blow that horn but I could never do it ... not enough wind then. This was the early 1940s and my father worked here for the A.N.D. Company until his death in 1949.

There was not much for my sister and me to do when we lived at the Staff House. The hall upstairs had a large hole in the floor about the size of a kitchen table, covered with a grate. Lavinia and I would lie on our bellies and look down. We could see the big stove. My father and the two cookees would be frying eggs, dozens of eggs, pancakes, and toutons made from bread dough. Dinnertime we saw potatoes and meat cooked. The meat was probably moose or pork. Pigs were raised for slaughter and, of course, moose was always available. We could also see and smell the mounds of fresh bread and molasses buns.

Our favourite entertainment was looking through the big hole in the floor. We didn't need TV. We would wait for the forty to sixty men to come in from the woods. The number depended on the time of the year. Then the fun began as they ate and joked with one another, often bursting into gales of laughter. Lavinia and I strained to hear what was being said but we often didn't understand the loud chatter.

If we moved around the hole on our bellies we could see different parts of the room, the long tables and all the food. One day, one of us, accidentally or intentionally, threw a tiny piece of paper down the hole. We watched as it swayed down and stayed airborne over my father's head while he was cooking. The heat from the stove kept it in the air. It finally landed on his head. He didn't notice, but my mother saw it. Soon we heard loud footsteps on the stairs—we had been caught. Both of us were sent to our room.

My sister was lucky because she had to go to school. I practiced pick-up sticks. I always tried to beat my sister, but I never did. That incident did not, however, stop us from enjoying our daily entertainment.

I will take the blame for throwing the tiny piece of paper down the big hole because my sister passed away a few years ago and cannot defend herself. The men went home on weekends but if it was stormy and the roads were blocked with snow they had to stay at the depot. That made my sister and me happy because we had entertainment all weekend.

My sister, mother, and father have all passed on. However, some of my best memories are of the year we all lived up the depot.

Marjorie Fudge
MOUNT PEARL

❦ The Listening Post ❧

My first year teaching was in 1955-56 in a small rural community on Random Island, Trinity Bay. I was seventeen years of age and had just completed six weeks of summer school at Prince of Wales College, St. John's. The teaching conditions were such that almost any position was available with this level of education.

When I reached my destination in September, I got to know my boarding mistress and her family. Showing me around she said, "Now, there's a hole in the middle of your bedroom, which is right over the kitchen. The wood stove, our only source of heat, is directly under the hole. That will give you heat when you want it, but if it gets too warm pull your trunk over the hole."

"Will do," I said.

Things were going well. I became good friends with a girl who was about the same age as me. Her boyfriend came to my boarding house one night while she was visiting. After lunch was served, I decided to go to bed early, giving my friend some time alone with her boyfriend.

After some time I got curious and decided to pull the trunk off the hole in my bedroom. In my pajamas, I knelt on the floor and bent with eyes and ears to the hole. It was too dark in the kitchen to see much but I heard talking from the daybed area. I listened for awhile.

A couple of days later, as we walked to another community, I told her what I did and especially what I heard.

She said, "You devil! I won't be courting there anymore."

And she didn't.

That was my balcony view fifty-five years ago.

Reta Phillips
Clarenville

❧ Scars ❧

I was about eighteen months old at the time and the year was 1944. We were living in Nova Scotia. We had one of those holes in the ceiling and it was right above the wood stove. I was upstairs with my sister, who probably was supposed to be looking after me. She was twelve years older.

Being that young I guess I didn't know much about danger, so there I was with my feet dangling down through the hole. Pretty soon down I went—unfortunately for me, there was a full dinner cooking on the stove.

I bounced off the warming oven on top and landed right on the cooking dinner. My dear mother, God rest her soul, was at the kitchen table and heard the great crash.

She came running over and put her hands under me and lifted me off the stove and no doubt saved my life. She had a butcher knife in her hand but I guess she didn't think of that. I shudder to think of what she could have done with that. Until the day she died she had scars on the back of her hands and I still have a scar on my elbow (reportedly from a pot of carrots) and a scar on the bottom of my right bicep.

This story has been in my family all these years, but I don't remember it—it was all related to me by my mother and sister.

Eric White
Cape Broyle

Cooking Lessons

I was only twelve years old when Mom became so ill she had to stay in bed for almost a year and I, the oldest of four children, had to stay home from school to cook and clean for the family. My father worked in the Bell Island mines and did some fishing and farming. He worked hard to keep us all together.

We used coal and I remember he used to bank the stove at night. There was a hole in the dining room ceiling, which was under their bedroom to let the heat up to keep Mom warm. Mom said she could feel the heat rising.

Mom taught me to cook through that hole. I would keep going into the dining room to ask her how to do things. I learned to make bread. She would tell me to put the cake of yeast in soak, put the flour through the sieve into the bowl, and hand mix it in the bread pan until I could hear her saying, "That's enough." Then I would cover the bread pan with blankets for the night and place it near the chimney for heat, so it would rise and be ready to shape and place in small, greased pans. The next morning, the dough would have to rise again before being baked in the oven.

Sometimes I brought the whole works up to show her. She always said, "That's beautiful." She was a very diplomatic woman. It made me eager to work harder.

I also liked to look at the beautiful Christmas tree from there. Every year, I got a good view of the old crepe paper Santa, with his cardboard boots, as he took his place on top of the tree. I spent many hours there, probably because I was also close to Mom.

What I didn't hear at the hole was talk of the sinking of boats during the war, the explosions we witnessed, and the bodies we saw. We knew it must have been discussed among the grownups, but, listen as we might, we children never heard it mentioned while listening at the hole. Makes me think my parents knew we had big ears.

The house was later sold and torn down after the mines closed.

Ron Hammond
Bell Island

❧ Moving In ☙

My earliest memory that I can reliably date involves a hole in the kitchen ceiling.

Late in the fall of 1958, Mom and Dad moved into a house they had rented "up the Motion" in Clarke's Beach. The day we moved in, I remember sitting on the floor in the kitchen alongside Dad. He was putting our cook stove together. Most likely, I wasn't much help. I remember it was chilly until Dad got the stove together and a good wood fire going.

Mom, who was pregnant with my sister, was putting things away upstairs in the bedroom. She could talk to us as she looked down into the kitchen through the hole in the ceiling.

This was only a few months before my third birthday. However, there were many times when we were small that my sister and I looked down into the kitchen through the heat vent over the stove. While other memories over the next seven or eight years come to mind, none is as clear as the day we moved in and Dad got the house warm and cozy. I felt welcomed to our new home.

Gary Snow
St. John's

❧ Shortcut ❦

About sixty years ago, I lived in a house off Fleming Street and we had a hole in the kitchen ceiling. The hole went up to our parents' bedroom from the kitchen and not only served as a method to heat the upstairs but also a great way to communicate to anyone who was down in the kitchen. We could just stick our heads down the hole and talk to someone without having to go downstairs.

My eldest sister was responsible for cleaning the rooms upstairs. While she was busy cleaning, our mischievous seven-year-old brother was always getting in her way. One day, he bugged her so much, she grabbed him by the arms and stuck him down the hole. After a few seconds he screamed in terror, so she pulled him up. Needless to say she never had a problem with him again, but she had to answer to my mother. My sister got a scolding for doing such a terrible thing to her brother.

Gerry Sulley
St. John's

❧ Give Us This Day ... ☙

I was the youngest of five children. My mother died when I was four years old. Dad raised the five of us on his own. We had a big two-storey house on a large farm in Holyrood. I often think of how cold it was in the morning when I stepped out of bed. I also remember having a pee pot under the bed.

The thing that sticks in my memory was the hole in the ceiling. I spent a lot of time there, mostly listening to what was going on. I was being quite nosy actually. Most of what I heard was everyday talk, neighbours and relatives dropping in to chat. I couldn't see a lot because the hole was directly over the stove and my view was limited. I could see, however, the end of the couch, which was by the kitchen stove.

What I saw there one morning has stayed with me over the years and been a great sense of comfort for me. Dad was a big strong man who farmed for a living. There he was kneeling on the floor, his elbows on the couch, his head in his hands, saying his prayers before he started the day.

We talk about things in life which influence the way we live and something as simple as this has strongly influenced mine.

Phyllis Mary Smith
Kelligrews

Fishing through the Hole

It was a late spring evening in Williamsport on the Great Northern Peninsula. At ten and eleven years old, we flamers (rascal, hard case), my sister and I, were sent upstairs to bed. We could hear our friends playing outside on the bridge that ran past our two-storey house. We were bored and mischievous as we tried to figure out what to do.

As I glanced across the room, I spied a piece of plywood covering the hole in the floor of my bedroom where my father had earlier removed a stovepipe.

"Let's go fishin'!" I said to my sister, who quickly and gingerly slid the piece of plywood off the hole. I proceeded to retrieve some fishhooks and string from my brigs pocket.

Underneath the hole sat my oldest sister, who was studying for her public exams. She was sitting in a large comfy armchair, with her math set lying on a doily on the wide arm of the chair. The protractor, compass, and ruler seemed to wink at us as the late evening sun glinted through the kitchen window, reflecting off the metal objects. Our sister was oblivious to the two rascals peering down from the hole in the ceiling, as she worked intently on her projects.

I did the first cast with the large fish hook ... down ... down ... down it went. As I pulled back, it hooked into the large holes of the rose pattern doily, causing the math set to spill across the hard linoleum floor with a great ruckus.

Our sister was spooked! We could hear her screaming for our mother as we slammed back the plywood cover and dove into the bed expecting to get a tongue-lashing or thrashing.

The community was later resettled. We moved in 1965. The following year my father disassembled the house and carried it to Englee, seventeen miles up the coast, to use in the construction of a new one.

Guy Randell
St. John's

～ The Peep Hole in the Ceiling ～

AUGH, THE HOLE IN the ceiling or the floor, depending on from which angle you viewed it, for me brings back childhood memories. This unique hole was usually found near the centre of the house, alongside the chimney, which normally was situated in the centre of the home, so as the heat from the wood stove could be distributed evenly to the upstairs rooms. Manys a time I overnighted at either Aunt Lindy's or Aunt Pauline's houses that were two storeys high and would be lucky enough to be paired with the occupant who slept in the bedroom with the "peep" hole. This room was the toastiest in the winter and the sweatiest in the summer, depending on what time of year you were there for a sleepover.

My most memorable recollection of the hole stems from an experience at our family home in Seal Cover, a bungalow, not during a sleepover. Now, why or how, you are probably thinking to yourself, would the hole be utilized in a bungalow? Well, to be sure, our bungalow did not have a peep hole; at least, not intentionally.

Our bungalow was home to Dad, Mom, my brother, and me. As in most bungalows, the brick chimney was located in the centre of the house and the only source of heat a combination coal-wood-oil stove in the kitchen. Later, two sisters, Carrie and Trinalynn, were added to our family, but, by that time, our home had been remodelled into a larger bungalow with central heating in the form of an oil furnace.

One day when my brother and I were enjoying summer holidays, we were all in the kitchen while Mom was cooking supper. She had a roaring fire going in the stove. Unbeknownst to any of us, there was a spray can of air freshener on the warmer. The warmer was the shelf above the stove which held mitts for drying, steel wool for cleaning the stovetop, and small pots for cooking. The top ledge was used to lodge items as the need arose.

The heat from the fire in the stove built up such pressure inside the aerosol that it shot up through the Donna Conna ceiling like a rocket ship. A gigantic BANG was heard above the stove. There was now a hole in the ceiling where there wasn't one before. When Dad returned home, he retrieved the can of air freshener from the attic. The warmer was never again used as a storage shelf.

Madonna M. Rideout
CONCEPTION BAY SOUTH

The Dance

In the early 1950s, we young ones heard of a concert on Ireland's Eye Island. A crowd of us got in a boat on a cold windy November night and headed for Ivanhoe, where the concert was going ahead. After the concert, which was only about a half-hour long, the dance started.

During the dance a young fellow from Ivanhoe invited our boyfriends to come with him for a drink, which was not unusual during outport dances. Off they chased this young fellow, who was about fifteen or sixteen years old. He took them to his home, where he planked a bottle on the table. More than likely it was moonshine. The kitchen was full of people telling stories and singing songs. Our boyfriends told us they didn't know anything before this older man with a three-day beard poked his head down the hole, above the stove. From his vantage point he insisted, "Put MY bottle on the table and have a swalley on me."

There were lots of hoots and hollers. It seems that the old fellow had been barred from the dance the week before for fighting and his wife only allowed him out of bed, as far as the hole, that night.

Annie and Reg King
CLARENVILLE

❧ Spies ☙

I was born and raised in the tiny community of Small Point in Conception Bay North in 1958, so I know well about the hole. Ours was in the kitchen and rendered heat to the bedroom above, but my five siblings and I never saw this as a heat source but a great way to be a voyeur to everything going on in the tiny kitchen below.

I can well remember the mornings, peeking through the hole to see if our mother was finished her breakfast, as this was probably the only time in the day that she was permitted to sit quietly and enjoy her cup of tea. She would have to listen to the litany of "Mommy can we come down, Mommy can we come down …" This was all voiced through the hole in the kitchen ceiling.

I also remember vividly when my grandmother would visit from Northern Bay, where she lived with her daughter. We would listen intently through the hole to the hushed tones of their voices. Perhaps there would be a little idle gossip or a discussion about a sick relative or maybe about the birth of a new baby. That four-inch hole allowed us to peek into the lives of people we probably didn't even know.

I also have dear memories of watching my father, who passed away in 1966 at the age of forty. I could see him drinking his tea and smoking a cigarette.

Today with Facebook and Twitter we seek and peek into the lives of family, friends, and people with whom we are only barely familiar. Having a hole in the kitchen ceiling allowed family to witness what was going on in the home long after you went to bed. Perhaps a kiss from your parents, a tear silently falling remembering a loved one. This left heartwarming memories in your mind forever.

Peggy Doyle
BURNT POINT, CONCEPTION BAY

Found Out

I lived in an older home in Winterton, Trinity Bay, that had a ceiling hole in my parent's bedroom. I know that the purpose of that hole was to allow heat from the kitchen stove to heat this bedroom.

For me, though, the real purpose of that hole was to peep down to see what was going on downstairs when I was supposed to be in bed.

I am the youngest of five children. Because of this, I was sent to bed early, while the others could stay up later. I felt I was being deprived. Although I looked down into the kitchen, this was unbeknownst to my family. Maybe it wasn't as exciting as I thought. One night, my father found me asleep by the hole. I was found out and that ended my peeping days.

My parents are long gone to Heaven, but my siblings and I treasure those memories.

Rosalie Quinn (nee Hiscock)
Clarke's Beach

Yeast and Malt

As a young girl growing up in Adam's Cove, Conception Bay, during the 1940s and 50s, the kitchen stove was the only source of heat for our entire house. Often the heat generated from cooking and baking bread in the cast iron stove became intense. Hence, the hole in the ceiling.

I was the only girl in our family of four children. I slept in the small bedroom, which happened to be above the kitchen and therefore had the sought-after hole. Because of this my bedroom was always warm, even in winter. However, the hole served other purposes as well. I remember that many cups of water were passed through the hole to me and my thirsty brothers. The hot water bottle and heated beach rocks were also passed up through the hole to heat our beds.

I listened to such stories as *The Cisco Kid* and *Hopalong Cassidy* from our kitchen radio. I could listen to the stories even after my bedtime when I wasn't allowed back in the kitchen.

At that time, especially in the winter, it seemed that everything was stored in the kitchen. I could see the woodbox, coal bucket, coats, boots, and mittens hung to dry. All had to be ready for us to wear to school the next morning. What didn't fit there was often stored in my warm bedroom. Because of the hole in the ceiling, the heat warmed many a keg of home brew and moonshine. My room was a suitable place to hide those illegal activities. But then my father always turned out a good batch of brew. No wonder that many a night I fell asleep with the pleasant smell of yeast and malt in my nostrils, thanks to the hole in the ceiling.

Judy Shortt
HOLYROOD

The Secret

As a child growing up in Corner Brook with my one brother, George, I remember my grandfather making a hole in the ceiling over the kitchen stove. Upstairs, the hole was in the hallway leading to the bedrooms. It was to drive heat upstairs in the winter months. As well, the heat dried the laundry Mom and Grandma hung on the clothesline in the hall. Grandpa had put up the clothesline from one end of the hall to the other to be used mostly in the winter months when it was too cold and stormy to hang clothes outside.

The hole was my favourite place to listen to stories being told by adults in the kitchen.

One Christmas Eve, when I was about seven or eight years old, I saw Mom and Grandma taking our Christmas toys to the Christmas tree to fill our stockings. What a shock to learn there was no Santa Claus.

Although I did not tell Mom or Grandma what I saw, I did tell my brother. He and I kept our secret for a long time, though I'm not sure whether it was so that we would not upset Mom, or whether we just wanted to keep the presents coming!

Beulah Gillingham (nee Locke)
Burlington, Ontario

Acknowledgements

Thank you to all the contributors to this book. Without their curiosity, sense of preservation, and input, this book would not have happened.

Garry Cranford of Flanker Press was especially available to support any requests and provide input.

Angela Otto, Judy Lawlor, and Paul Butler readily provided assistance by judging the story contest upon request.

Thanks to Ed Roche, Samantha Galway, Lisa Galway, Joanne Hann, Ed and Gail Snook for helping make the painting *Balcony View* a reality. As well, thanks to Guy Randell at the Art and Frame Shop for encouraging me to collect other stories when he related his "story on the spot."

Thanks to my sister, Ellen Conway, "partner in crime" at the hole; my brother, John D. Brazil, for his critique of Mom's Story; and, Jeff Galway and Lori Galway for their interest and support.

As always, thanks to Michael Galway, Peggy Herring, and their son Devin for professional and personal assistance from the conception to completion of this collection of stories.

My appreciation to my friends, the Bookbags, for listening to the stories while housebound during Hurricane Igor.

Special thanks to my husband, John, for encouraging me to stay the course, and doing whatever was necessary to fulfill my dream to preserve this little corner of our Newfoundland heritage.

This book of stories began with my parents, Michael Brazil, Mary Cooney, and Dennis Cooney. Their gifts to me of a sense of home, security, and humour piqued my interest in the hole in the kitchen ceiling. This book is dedicated to their memory.

Anne Galway grew up in North River, Conception Bay. Since retiring from the education profession, she has been a writer and visual artist focusing on the landscape and culture of Newfoundland and Labrador.

Her memoir articles have appeared in periodicals such as *Downhome* magazine. She also writes poetry and is a member of the Writer's Guild of Newfoundland and Labrador and the Writers' Alliance of Newfoundland and Labrador.

Her visual art appears in local art venues and churches, as well as in private collections across Canada. Her well-known painting *Balcony View* was used as the basis of the cover of this story collection.

Anne's experience as a teacher and guidance counsellor spans thirty years in many Newfoundland communities, including St. John's, Gander, Corner Brook, and Codroy Valley. However, her most treasured educational experiences relate back to the hole in the kitchen ceiling. She can still hear her mother admonishing her: "Anne, get away from the hole and into bed," which sometimes (but not often) deterred her from this pastime. Aware she had not been the only one receiving the benefit of this education, she encouraged over one hundred contributors to record their experiences in *Stories from the Hole in the Ceiling*.

Her next book will be about a young girl's adventure when she visited Labrador as a member of a Newfoundland fishing family in the early 1930s.

Anne lives in St, John's, Newfoundland and Labrador, with her husband, John. *Stories from the Hole in the Ceiling* is her first book.

Index of Contributors

Antle, Darlene 106
Barnes, Rick 20
Bedingfield, Dolores 109
Belcher, Ina 15
Bennett, J. Pius 129
Bennett, JoAnna 48
Billard, Marilyn 81
Breen, Peter 117
Brennan, Barbara 58
Brown, Owen 137
Cantwell, Theresa 90
Chaulk, Ethel 53
Colbourne, Rex 43
Collins, Gary 138
Croft, Lorraine 150
Croke, Isabel 147
Dalton, Gordon 120
Dewling, Clarence and Sarah 77
Dominix, A. 152
Doyle, Peggy 173
Drake, Maryanne 89
"Esau" 14
Finn, Alice Lee 93
Fitzgerald, Dorothy 87
Fournier, Louise 25
Frampton, Vera Riggs 114

Fudge, Marjorie 160
Galway, Anne 1, 63, 124
George, Pearl 11, 149
Gillingham, Beulah 176
Gladney, Jolene 36
Goodyear, Minnie 54
Hammond, Ron 165
Holwell, Jeanette 136
Hynes, Dolores 7
Inkpen, Beulah 27
Kean, Mabel 1, 101
Kean, Patricia 122
Kear, Celine Power 56
Keating, Eileen 145
Kelly, Donna Marie 12, 96
Keough, Geraldine 50
King, Annie and Reg 172
King, Daphne 121
Lee, Dolo 35
Lee, Kathy 115
Lopez, T. 10
Macpherson, Joyce and Alan 91
Malarsky, Donna Judge 105
Martin, Emma 80
Martin, Paul 44
McDonald, Agatha 59

McHugh, Gloria J. 118
Morgan, Beulah 28
Norman, Ed 140
Otto, Angela 51
Pardy, Phillip 75
Peddle, Connie 157
Peddle, Erika 16
Peddle, Rhonda 131
Pender, Anita 1, 85
Peters, Catherine 18
Phillips, Reta 163
Pilgrim-Simms, Sherry 37
Power, Patricia 111
Pumphrey, Ron 29
Quinn, Rosalie 174
Randell, Guy 169
Rideout, Madonna M. 170
Ridgley, Elizabeth 123
Roberts, Joseph W. 92
Rorke, John 19
Ryan, Betty 23
Ryan, Maureen 47
Shears, Steven and Dallis 113
Shortt, Judy 175
Smith, Phyllis Mary 168
Snook, Gail 94
Snow, Gary 166
Strong, Tony 135
Sturge, George J. 148
Sulley, Gerry 167
Thornhill, Foster 24
Tippett, Myrtle 142
Unsigned, 42
Walker, Anne Murrin 112
Walsh (Aucoin), Dianne 79

Walsh, Mary (Collins) and Doris Collins-Scott 83, 84
White, Eric 164
Willmott, Roger 132
Winsor, Donna 144